THINKING STRATEGICALLY

A Primer for Public Leaders

THINKING STRATEGICALLY

A Primer for Public Leaders

Susan Walter & Pat Choate

BERTRAM WAKELEY, PROJECT MANAGER
JUYNE KAUPP LINGER, EDITOR
NORMA deFREITAS, PRODUCTION MANAGER

THE COUNCIL OF STATE PLANNING AGENCIES
HALL OF THE STATES
400 NORTH CAPITOL STREET
WASHINGTON DC 20001

© 1984 by the Council of State Planning Agencies

Library of Congress Cataloging in Publication Data

Walter, Susan, 1947-
  Thinking Strategically.

  Bibliography: p.
  Includes index.
  1. Administrative agencies—United States—Planning.
  2. Public administration—United States—Planning.
  3. Corporate planning—United States.   I. Choate, Pat.
  II. Title.
  JK421.W35 1984   353'.072   84–15544
  ISBN 0-934842-19-1

Cover Design by Donya Melanson Associates
Typography by The TypeWorks

Manufactured in the United States

The Council of State Planning Agencies is a membership organization comprised of the planning and policy staff of the nation's governors. Through its Washington office, the Council provides assistance to individual states on a wide spectrum of policy matters. The Council also performs policy and technical research on both state and national issues. The Council has been affiliated with the National Governors' Association since 1975.

The Council of State Planning Agencies
Hall of States
400 North Capitol Street
Washington, D.C. 20001
(202) 624-5386

James M. Souby
Executive Director

Authors' Biographies

SUSAN WALTER is Manager for State Government Issues at the General Electric Company. Prior to joining General Electric, Ms. Walter was the Associate Director for Executive Management of The Council of State Planning Agencies.

Ms. Walter has had diverse experience in the analysis and management of public policy issues for both the legislative and executive branches of government. She was the primary staff person for the White House Conference on Strategic Planning and edited its *Proceedings.* She co-authored *America in Ruins* with Pat Choate and was the General Editor for *The Game Plan: Governance with Foresight.*

Before her association with The Council of State Planning Agencies, Ms. Walter was a Special Assistant to Governor Reubin Askew and the Executive Director of the Florida Advisory Council on Intergovernmental Relations. In addition, she has held senior staff positions for both the Florida House of Representatives and Senate in human services and appropriations.

Ms. Walter received her masters degree from the Maxwell School of Syracuse University.

PAT CHOATE has worked in policy and administrative positions with the United States Department of Commerce and the State governments of Tennessee and Oklahoma. He has written extensively about education and training, public infrastructure, economic development, and management. He is the co-author with Susan Walter of *America in Ruins.* He holds a Ph.D. in economics from the University of Oklahoma and is the Senior Policy Analyst for Economics at TRW Inc. in Washington, D.C.

Acknowledgment

THE VARIOUS DRAFTS of this book have been reviewed by many individuals. Many of these people are in sensitive positions, thus, to list them would take advantage of their frankness and their contributions. However, their thoughtful and often provocative observations are appreciated.

The appendix contains abstracts from a special report prepared for the Congress by a group of business executives. The lexicon of terms in the appendix draws heavily on that report. We appreciate the time that several of the authors of that report have given us.

Several other individuals were most helpful including Robert Wise, Ray Ewing, Walter Hahn, Ken Hunter, John Clough, Dennis Little, and Jim Souby. We are particularly appreciative of the support and counsel of Ed Kelly, Norma deFreitas and the staff at the Council.

Juyne Linger, our editor, merits special recognition. She made a very special contribution through her insights and the clarity that she brought to this book. We very much appreciate her efforts.

We appreciate most the support given to us by J. Jackson Walter and Diane C. Choate. Once again, their good humor and encouragement helped enormously.

And as always, the authors assume sole responsibility for any errors of fact or interpretation contained herein.

Special Acknowledgment

BERTRAM F. WAKELEY was monitor of this project for the Council of State Planning Agencies. Throughout the research and writing of this book, he gave us support, encouragement and assistance. He challenged us to focus on the pragmatic dimensions of how to pursue excellence in government management. He was generous with his time, knowledge and experiences in State Government. He reviewed the many drafts, made numerous suggestions and was always patient. Bert, we appreciate your many contributions and your good spirit. Thanks.

TABLE OF CONTENTS

LIST OF FIGURES

Introduction

MANAGEMENT IS AN ABSTRACT PROCESS, visible primarily in its results—good or bad. Today, those results suggest serious shortcomings in management processes across the spectrum of American society. In the private sector, management deficiencies have contributed to declining productivity, lagging competitiveness and lost markets. In the public sector, they are a primary source of government's inability to perform adequately even basic functions such as maintaining the public infrastructure, providing adequate public education and assuring the public safety.

Some management deficiencies are a consequence of poor administrative procedures. But many others reflect a more fundamental and critical management weakness: a lack of strategic vision to guide decisions and actions. Indeed, most organizations make no systematic effort to anticipate and understand influential trends and events that are likely to affect them. Nor do they cultivate an explicit, shared understanding of the nature and purpose of the organization. And even when an organization is able to create a strategic vision, it often has no systematic means of translating that vision into specific plans and actions.

Fortunately, many leaders in both business and government have begun to recognize and respond to this need for a systematic long-term view. A number of major corporations have been successful in analyzing their current and future environments, in creating a strategic vision based on those analyses, and in shaping their goals, plans and operations to fit that vision. So too, several forward-thinking governors, Members of Congress and federal Cabinet officials have demonstrated how a clear strategic vision can improve decision-making and program administration in the public sector. Systematic foresight, coupled with the creation of clear, long-term goals and strategic plans, motivates and guides these organizations, enabling them to minimize uncertainties, maximize opportunities and, at the same time, provide greater organizational stability in these unsettled times.

As applied by leading private and public organizations, this process of foresight, goal-setting and strategic planning creates a qualitatively different perspective on the future, beyond a simple extrapolation of current events. Rather, the process treats the future as a product of today's decisions.

Peter Drucker observes that long-range planning does not deal with future decisions, but rather with the futurity of present decisions. As Drucker explains, "The question that faces the long-range planner is not what we should do tomorrow. It is: what do we have to do today to be ready for an uncertain tomorrow? The question is not what will happen in the future. It is: what futurity do we have to factor into our present thinking and doing, what time spans do we have to consider, and how do we converge them to a simultaneous decision in the present?"[1]

The purpose of this book is to describe the principles that leading private and public organizations employ to create a strategic vision; to examine specific techniques they are using; and to explain how these techniques can be replicated. This work is organized in four parts:

- Part I describes pivotal management challenges facing both the private and public sectors;
- Part II describes how a clear understanding of the "futurity" of present decisions can shape the political environment in which organizations function;
- Part III presents a framework for creating a systematic foresight, goal-setting and strategic planning process; and
- Part IV describes principles and techniques that federal, state and local officials can apply in creating and implementing a strategic vision for their institutions.

Although this work is aimed primarily at managers in the public sector, the principles and processes described are applicable to managers of virtually every type of organization, large or small, for profit or nonprofit.

CHAPTER ONE

The Management Challenges

Shared Challenges

TODAY, THE MANAGEMENT CHALLENGES facing the Chief Executive Officers (CEOs) of corporations and the Chief Elected Officials (CEOs) of government are remarkably similar. For example, both face:

- overwhelming pressures to favor the short term over the long term, irrespective of eventual consequences;
- problems of managing large, often unresponsive bureaucracies;
- internal and external forces that resist change, regardless of how much that change is required;
- pressures of special interest groups—often the same special interest groups;
- difficulties in finding and retaining creative, productive people;
- the problems of creating or finding new ideas and new approaches;
- the difficulties of sharing decisions with individuals and institutions outside of the organization; and
- the problems of securing and allocating limited funds for virtually unlimited demands.

The similarity of the management challenges shared by public and private organizations extends beyond the apparently generic problems of managing large bureaucracies. Many of the same external forces affect the environments in which both public and private organizations operate. For example, in its 1980 report, *Looking Ahead,* the Committee for Economic Development (CED) identified some of the key issues that business will face in the 1980s.[2]

Among the issues identified were changes in demography and the labor force; the changing character of work; growing international dependence; a new public questioning of economic decisions; inflation; taxes; government regulation; the changing social role of business; increased competition for capital; the decline of many traditional industries and the resulting loss of jobs; and the problems of maintaining fiscally sound retirement programs. Each of these business issues is a government issue as well.

Similarly, in its 1983 report, *Future Opportunities and Problems That Face the Nation*, the Committee on Energy and Commerce of the U.S. House of Representatives identified 10 basic, long-term issues now confronting the nation.[3] Among the issues identified were changes in the labor force, international trade, information technology, governmental institutions, education, natural resources and food scarcity, public facilities, armaments, research and development, and health care. Each of these government issues is also a business issue.

Some examples illustrate the similarity of issues that confront CEOs and institutions in both the public and private sectors:

- *The Work Force*—The growth in the size of the American work force is slowing dramatically. As a result, today's workers will constitute over 80 percent of the work force in the year 2000. The nation's success in renewing its economy will therefore depend heavily on how well the *current* work force can be retrained and upgraded. Workers for both government and business will come from this same pool of workers.[4]

  The future status and role of labor unions remain unclear, as unions seek to offset membership losses in older industries by expanding into services, high technology and other largely non-unionized industries.

  Women will constitute almost two of every three new entrants into the work force until the mid-1990s. Yet no major institution in America, public or private, has effectively integrated women into its work force.

  Disruptions in the work place are likely as the workers of the post-World War II baby-boom generation compete for mid-career promotions.

- *Trade and Investment*—The United States economy is intricately entwined with the global economy. Increasingly, the U.S. performance in the global economy is influenced by access to markets, competitive financing and the "industrial targeting" strategies of other nations. Even though trade will become increasingly important in the years ahead, world and U.S. trade policies and mechanisms are inadequate: the General Agreement on Trade and Tariffs does not include trade in services, which contributes $120 billion to the American economy each year; the safeguard codes which provide remedies for tariff violations are threadbare and ineffective; the U.S. lacks basic information about the trade and investment practices of other nations; and our trading partners are applying a wide range of unfair non-tariff trade and investment barriers against American products and services.

- *Public Infrastructure*—The deterioration of the nation's basic public facilities is extensive. Adequate and well-functioning roads, bridges, water and wastewater treatment systems, ports, school buildings, libraries, parks and community buildings, among dozens of other types of public works, are essential to the U.S. economy and the quality of life of every citizen. Yet the national, state and local governments have few policies or programs to address this fundamental challenge: priorities do not exist; adequate funding mechanisms have not been created; research is limited, almost nonexistent; public decision-making is fragmented between and among the federal and state governments; and there are no clear divisions of responsibilities between the public and private sectors.

- *Information Technologies*—Today, information technologies affect most aspects of human activity, including health, defense, politics and education. The pervasiveness of these technologies has created a range of critical issues that need to be addressed. Abroad, other governments are erecting barriers to the movement of information across borders, impeding U.S. investment overseas. Domestically, the ability to access and use information is magnifying the gap between segments of society. The extensive information now available on businesses and individuals has created an urgent need to safeguard privacy. Yet neither the government nor most corporations have adequate policies to deal with these important information issues.

- *Government Institutions*—Government institutions have become cumbersome. Specifically, it has become increasingly difficult to build a consensus on basic issues; the debate on centralization versus decentralization of government proceeds more on the basis of rhetoric than from a clear understanding of alternatives and consequences; electoral processes leave citizens feeling powerless, stimulating referendum movements that are sweeping state governments; and the relationship between government, business and labor remains confrontational, even while the need for cooperation becomes ever more critical.

- *Education*—The nation's education system is in decline. A growing number of reports have documented the inadequacies of public education, from kindergarten through high school. At the college level, the skills of new graduates do not match the needs of society. Nor do public training programs meet the nation's retraining needs. Indeed, because strategic vision is absent at every level of education and training, deficiencies exist in pay, faculty, facilities, curriculum, and linkages with America's needs.

- *Natural Resources and Food*—The United States and its allies remain dependent on oil imports and are vulnerable to supply disruptions. Globally, over 800 million people consume less than the accepted minimum daily caloric requirement. In addition, America's growing dependence on strategic materials found only in nations such as Zaire, Zimbabwe, South Africa and the Soviet Union poses a serious threat to our economy and national security.

  Domestically, the availability of potable water is a major national problem that is certain to worsen. During the next two decades, for example, the depletion of underground water sources in the High Plains states of Texas, Oklahoma, Nebraska, Kansas, New Mexico and Colorado will force most farmers to return to the low-yield dry-land farming that existed in the 1930s. Consequently, more than 25 percent of all irrigated farm production in the United States will cease. Since these farms currently produce over 40 percent of the nation's beef, changes in U.S. diets and food supply are inevitable.

- *Armaments*—The stockpile of world armaments is at record levels and arms are increasingly being diffused among less developed nations, with obvious destabilizing effects. In addition to ongoing arms negotiations, the next decade is likely to witness the emergence of related issues such as the safety of chemical and biological weapons during production, transport and storage; America's participation in efforts to curtail international terrorism; and the need for additional policymaking mechanisms on national security.

- *Research and Development*—Research and development (R&D), coupled with technological innovation, have long been mainstays of America's competitive edge. But current trends indicate a decline in U.S. innovation relative to our past performance and to that of our foreign competitors. In spite of the importance of government funding of basic R&D and government's central role in regulating and protecting improved technological innovations, the nation lacks a comprehensive policy for R&D and industrial innovation and technology. Consequently, business perceptions of government actions remain clouded.

- *Health Costs*—Even though health expenditures now exceed 10 percent of the Gross National Product, they are certain to escalate in the years ahead. As the population ages, these mounting health costs will place enormous demands on government, on employers who provide health benefit protection, and on individuals. Efforts to control health costs will force the nation to make critical choices about access to health care as well as the quality of services provided.

At the same time, the aging and increasing life expectancy of the population will create growing demands for particular kinds of health services such as acute and long-term health care. Changing migration patterns will determine where these demands will be most intense.

This is only a partial listing of foreseeable, long-term changes that will affect both government and business. In a world of global interdependencies and fast-paced change, it is imperative for organizations to anticipate the future, plan for it, and take considered action.

This is precisely why better managed corporations, and recently some governments as well, are applying the concepts of strategic vision: so that they can better understand and operate in their complex environments. The techniques, processes and tools of strategic vision enable these organizations to identify and analyze emerging trends and specific events that shape their working environment, define the basic objectives of their organizations, create strategic plans and link these plans to their day-to-day actions.

The Lack of Strategic Vision

The refinement and replication of the concepts of strategic vision that have evolved in the private sector hold enormous promise for improving the quality of management in government. And the quality of government management does require improvement.

The deficiencies in the quality of government management can be divided into two basic categories. The first are administrative, such as incompetencies in day-to-day operations, unresponsive service by many public employees, uninspired and thoughtless management by many government managers, poor purchasing procedures and slow decision-making.

The second are strategic deficiencies: the scant consideration given to identifying and assessing the consequences of longer-term trends and events, the absence of clear goals, poor or nonexistent strategic planning processes, limited linkages between plans and actions, and the absence of evaluation and feedback mechanisms.

As a consequence of both administrative and strategic deficiencies, American government today is managed as though government were somehow unimportant. The passage of legislation, announcement of policies, passage of appropriations, creation of programs, and issuance of rules and regulations are too often equated with actual accomplishment. But the chasm between intention and results is wide.

This is because management and results, per se, have been largely overlooked in both electoral politics and the actual conduct of the public's business. Consequently, virtually all of the 82,000 units of government in the United States operate without basic processes and tools for anticipating the future, preparing for its uncertainties or even operating coherently in the present.

If government really were unimportant, its mismanagement—administrative and strategic—would be of little consequence. But just the opposite is true. The federal, state and local governments influence virtually all economic and social decisions in the country through a diverse array of tax, expenditure and regulatory actions. Government now employs almost one of every six American workers and commands more than a third of the nation's annual Gross National Product. Government's decisions, actions and inactions affect the nation's economic performance, as well as its efforts to meet social objectives and maintain a secure national defense.

The mere reallocation of powers within the federalist system, per se, will not improve government management; nor will massive government reorganizations. (See Appendix A for a description of the techniques used most frequently to improve government management.) Improvement can come only from careful and pragmatic approaches that are deeply grounded in an understanding of the extent of the current ad hoc mismanagement, its causes, its consequences, and the actions required to facilitate change.

While the extent, consequences and costs of administrative deficiencies in the management of government have been documented repeatedly, the strategic deficiencies in government management are less clear. This is because strategic deficiencies are longer term in nature and are often masked and mislabeled as administrative weaknesses. The limited information that is available, however, outlines a disturbing situation in the strategic management of some fundamental areas of public-sector domestic responsibilities: managing the public work force, government expenditures, regulation and taxation. Some examples will illustrate the need for improved management in government—specifically, the need for more systematic foresight, goal-setting and strategic planning processes, as well as improved linkages between planning and operations and more effective evaluation procedures.

The Public Work Force

Virtually all decisions in U.S. society are affected, often substantially, by government workers. Thus, competent government management is essential to the effective functioning of society.

Yet the federal and state governments are permitting the career civil service to decline. At the same time, many competent, potential political appointees are unwilling to work in government because of low pay, high burnout rates and the high costs of moving and living in cities such as Washington, D.C.[5] Most disturbing, neither the federal nor the state and local governments have long-term policies to reverse the deterioration of the career service, attract a diversity of political appointees, or make public service attractive to well-qualified workers.

If the private sector chose its managers as government did, the CEO, the company president, all vice-presidents, all director-level managers and most plant managers would be fired and replaced at least every four to eight years. Most of their replacements would have little or no job-related experience or even professional training for these jobs. Under such circumstances, it might be difficult to manage a business successfully. Yet this is precisely how senior positions in the federal, state and local governments are staffed.

The turnover rate among the senior advisors to governors averages almost 33 percent annually.[6] At the federal level, during the past 14 years, there have been eight Secretaries of Commerce, seven Secretaries of State, and six Directors of the Office of Management and Budget. High turnover is found in every federal agency. Under these conditions, it is difficult to maintain continuity of programs.

In the past, high turnover among political officials at the federal level was offset by the relative permanence of senior career executives. But today, the unusually high level of resignations and retirements of these career officials threatens the effective functioning of government. Indeed, half of all senior executives—3,500 of the 7,000 highest level civil servants— have left the federal government since 1979.[7]

This crisis in government management is a direct, although unintended, consequence of the Civil Service Reform Act of 1978 which created the Senior Executive Service (SES). This system eliminated previous civil service protections, permitted flexibility in reassignments, and promised increased pay for outstanding work. But the system is a failure, at least in terms of its announced purposes. Specifically, the number of senior executives eligible for bonuses has been cut in half; reassignment authorities have been used to encourage the resignations of career officials; and career training has been reduced. Similar weaknesses are found in state governments as hundreds of state employees are fired with each change of administration.

The consequences of present practices are perhaps best stated by the Committee for Economic Development in their report, *Improving Management of the Public Work Force*:

> Some (public employees) are leaving for higher pay, prestige, or satisfaction in private employment; those whose jobs have few counterparts in the private sector feel caught and resentful; and many are resolved to fight through political action for what they perceive to be inadequate pay and working conditions. There are, in short, disturbing signs of sagging morale.[8]

As the CED points out, one of the most important considerations in managing government is the effective use of people. After all, government by its very nature is labor intensive; thus, improvements in the productivity of government services are heavily dependent on the improved management and performance of government workers.

Regulation

Government regulates banks and financial institutions, labor-management relations, public utilities, competition in the marketplace, communications, transportation, public safety, health, environment, entry into many professions, and a wide array of other activities that affect most citizens and all businesses.

In recent years, governmental regulation has become a major route for meeting social and economic objectives. Unable to generate sufficient grant-in-aid appropriations to finance social and economic programs in the 1970s, the federal and state governments expanded their regulatory powers and, in the process, shifted program costs to citizens, businesses and lower levels of government. Thus, while there were only 30 federal regulatory agencies in 1970, there were over 100 by 1980. A similar regulatory explosion occurred at the state level.

These regulations have imposed massive costs on business and even on government itself. In 1980, for example, businesses spent over $34 billion on air, water and solid waste pollution abatement, while government spent over $11.5 billion. Some of these requirements, such as provision of full access for the handicapped, would have literally bankrupted many local governments if implemented. Similarly, states have mandated that local governments take actions that have forced them to devise new ways of raising the necessary funds.[9]

Despite the obvious importance of some regulations and the unnecessary imposition of others, no reliable estimates of total regulatory costs and benefits exist. There is no overall focus for regulatory policies at the federal level; nor is there any coordination of regulatory policies among the federal, state and local agencies and those affected.

Government Expenditures

A lack of strategic vision, evident in massive waste, duplication and omission, also characterizes the more than $1 trillion of annual expenditures made by federal, state and local governments.

Consider, for example, the nation's outlays for public works. America's basic public facilities are wearing out faster than they are being repaired and replaced. Over $60 billion of public works expenditures are made annually in the absence of an inventory of public facilities, standards, uniform estimates of future investment requisites, or clear allocations of responsibilities. Although the deterioration of the nation's public facilities has been documented, only a few actions, such as the 5-cent gas tax, have been taken. Yet it is clear that continued deterioration of these basic facilities will suppress the vitality of the economy, reduce the quality of life of all citizens, and raise the costs of actions when they are eventually taken.[10]

An absence of strategic vision has also characterized the nation's employment and training policies, programs and institutions. Rapid technological advances and increased competition from abroad have created enormous demands for new and improved worker skills. At the same time, a growing segment of the work force is unprepared to meet these challenges. For example, a fifth of all American adults are functionally illiterate, unable to read a job notice, fill out a job application or make change correctly. Among adults who are unemployed, the rate of functional illiteracy is 36 percent.

Over $10 billion of federal, state and local funds is expended on public training programs each year. The training problem, therefore, is not a lack of money but rather the absence of a shared strategic vision of what should be done.

As a result, basic data on current and future training needs remain limited and of little use; training facilities are antiquated; faculty skills are becoming obsolete; and federal displaced worker retraining programs are fragmented in an ineffective maze of 22 distinct efforts. Furthermore, more than 20 states still have not established linkages between their training programs and employers—a technique pioneered by the southern states in their highly successful "customized" training programs which link specific worker training to the specific needs of specific employers.[11]

Taxation

The nation's tax system is confusing and ineffective. As much as $300 billion of the GNP may now be in the untaxed underground economy; the tax laws and regulations are so confusing that experts disagree on a growing number of points; most businesses and most citizens require expert assistance to complete their tax filings; and the level and nature of most economic investments are heavily influenced by their tax consequences.

Reductions of federal taxes in the "supply-side" economic experiment have had the effect of creating the largest deficit in the nation's history. As a result, the federal government has shifted many critical responsibilities to state and local governments. For unprepared state and local governments, these additional responsibilities have created difficult fiscal and administrative burdens that may take years to overcome.

But perhaps most important, the confusion of the nation's tax system, the growing perception of its unfairness, and the increasing visibility of unpunished tax cheaters are eroding the tax system's most precious asset: the good faith and voluntary compliance of American taxpayers.

The Consequences of Limited Vision

These examples are neither unique nor isolated. They simply illustrate the disorder that is created in the absence of foresight, goals, strategic plans, operations that are linked to plans, and regular evaluations. The absence of these basic public administration functions hamper government policies, institutions and programs in six basic ways:

1. *Fragmented and disordered management practices permit no overall view of public needs and no overall specification of the roles of the respective levels of government or the private sector in meeting those needs.* Without an ordered context for overall actions, a single decision cannot be considered relative to other decisions.

2. *In the absence of clearly documented needs and well-articulated priorities, pork-barrel politics often dominates public actions and public expenditures.* Pork-barrel spending becomes a medium of political exchange, in which votes and actions are exchanged for support of other programs or projects—regardless of public needs or benefits.

3. *In this atmosphere, the short-term payoff is invariably favored over long-term goals.* When public expenditures are treated as a source of patronage, it becomes difficult to create and maintain coalitions that can sustain long-term efforts, no matter how vital such efforts may be. As a result, most political leaders support those programs that can be financed and completed in a single year. Unfortunately, most of the nation's important challenges—such as rebuilding vital infrastructure, retraining the work force for jobs in a post-industrial society, assuring a safe environment, restoring long-term noninflationary economic growth, and rebuilding our defense capacities—will take a decade or more to finance and complete. Short-term approaches to such basic national needs will inevitably produce social and economic trauma.

4. *Without coherent strategies that set investment needs and ways to meet them, specific public investment plans for defense, social programs, research and development, and public facilities cannot be systematically formulated.* Nor can gov-

11

ernment leaders and the public determine critical linkages between various public functions, such as the role of employment and training in strengthening national defense capacities or the importance of public facilities to long-term economic growth.

5. *Disordered management practices at one level of government are easily transferred to other levels.* Thus, pork-barrel politics, a short-term perspective and start-and-stop financing at the federal level make it nearly impossible for state and local governments to plan and administer their responsibilities in a coherent manner.

6. *Disordered management practices in government limit, even prohibit, effective joint public-private sector actions.* Because of the costs, delays and bureaucracy involved, private firms often avoid doing business with government. The reluctance of private employers to participate in publicly sponsored training programs is only one of numerous examples of this fundamental breakdown between the principal institutions in American society.

The introduction of the techniques of strategic vision and management described in this book can be important first steps in bringing coherence to the management of government. Success in this effort, however, will require a thorough understanding of the forces that define the political environment in which government operates.

CHAPTER 2

The Politics

PRESIDENTS, GOVERNORS, MAYORS, county and other local officials operate at the intersection of the political world and the world of government management. Any attempt to improve the management of government must therefore recognize and accommodate the related political dimensions.

The reality and demands of the political process are an integral part of strategic vision and management in government. And strategic vision and strategic planning—along with the more thoughtful program administration they produce—are powerful tools that government leaders can use to deal effectively with the inevitable political forces they must manage if they are to be successful.

Politics, although often used as an excuse for poor government management, no more makes government unmanageable than competition and rapid change make businesses unmanageable. The particular arrangements of the American Republic—elections, federalism, separation of powers, the civil service system, short tenures of senior policymakers, special interest groups, an aggressive press and public participation—are as intrinsic to the public management environment as competitors, regulations, technical innovation, unions and export barriers are to the corporate environment.

And just as strategic management is tailor-made to the specific circumstances of those corporations where it has been used extensively and successfully, so too must it be tailored to the circumstances in which public institutions operate. Ideally, the strategic plan for government would not only include its political dimensions, but also *use* them to advance the goals of an administration.

Successful management of government, however, requires an understanding of the forces that shape the environment in which that management must proceed: the pressures of the perpetual campaign; transient leadership; special interest groups; the decline of political parties; governmental competition; the separation of powers; and the role of the media.

The Perpetual Campaign

The prime directive of political life is to get elected—and as often as possible. Most political leaders are almost continuously engaged in an election effort. President Carter, for example, began his campaign for the Presidency four years prior to his election in 1976. President Reagan ran for the Presidency in 1976 and again during the years between 1976 and 1980. The 1984 presidential campaign got under way in 1981 when prospective candidates began their "exploratory" efforts. Members of the Congress, governors and most local officials are similarly engaged in perpetual campaigns—a reality that is not likely to change.

In considering the effects of their decisions on the next election, government CEOs are not unlike business CEOs operating with an eye to the next quarterly report or stockholders meeting. Since elections occur less frequently than do annual stockholders meetings or the publication of annual reports, however, government leaders actually have a greater opportunity to take a long-term view than do many of their business counterparts and *more* time to anticipate and shape events and trends that would otherwise force short-term decisions.

In fact, most elected officials are quite effective in managing the time dimensions of their decisions. In the federal government, for example, difficult and politically unpopular decisions are generally made at the very beginning of an administration or at least postponed until after the midterm election. This practice is so prevalent that it has a working name—"presidential timing." Such timing is equally applicable in state and local governments.

The creation of a long-term vision with strategic plans and programs of implementation is an explicit means of managing the time dimensions of decisions. In the process, the pressures of the perpetual campaign are minimized, a longer term focus is created, and shorter term pressures are reduced.

Many states, for example, have established five- and seven-year planning and financing systems in transportation. The introduction of such plans in Pennsylvania, Oklahoma, California, Florida and Texas has not only eliminated many of the short-term pressures to use highway funds as a medium of political exchange, but also has permitted a longer term view and improved transportation management. New projects now are carefully and *openly* reviewed against other options, thus balancing political pressures. Most important, the time dimensions of decisions are shifted from the immediate to the longer term, an inevitable and desirable consequence of a strategic approach.

Transient Leadership

In the private sector, an orderly career path may extend for 30 years or more, perhaps culminating in five or more years as Chief Executive Officer. In government, by contrast, executive leadership changes often. President Eisenhower, for example, was the last President to serve two full terms.

The transient nature of public leadership, both elected and appointed, generates a number of basic difficulties in the long-term management of government. Government workers and potential sources of outside support are often unwilling to make long-term commitments to policies and programs linked to what are perceived as short-term public CEOs. Even if such policies and programs are implemented, moreover, they are likely to be altered or even eliminated by successors *unless* they enjoy wide support and are institutionalized.

Clearly, actions are required to minimize the disruptions of changing leadership. In part, such disruptions have been reduced by changes in many state constitutions permitting more than one term of office for governors. The processes of strategic vision and strategic management can help to strengthen leadership even further.

Systematic foresight—the analysis of emerging trends—can help secure agreement on circumstances and facts. Systematic goal-setting involving legislative bodies and outside groups can help secure agreement on the long-term basic objectives and priorities of an organization. Widely accepted long-term strategic plans can help assure the availability of resources and political support necessary for their implementation.

Special Interest Groups

Special interest groups are a modern political reality at every level of government. These groups of economic or social interests focus on a single issue or narrow group of issues in a well-organized and often well-financed manner. The number of these single-issue and special interest groups has grown almost in direct proportion and pace to government's expanding influence in the nation's economic and social affairs.

These special interest groups form one side of what is known as an "iron triangle"—that is, a mutually reinforcing network composed of parts of the public bureaucracy, parts of the legislative branch, and the special interest. One example of the hundreds of existing triangles is the network composed of the Department of Health and Human Services, the health industry and influential Members of Congress. This powerful triangle of mutual interests has been able to thwart federal efforts to reduce health costs despite the obvious need to do so.

During his first year in office, President Reagan demonstrated the power of a well-orchestrated plan when he overcame the influence of special interest groups opposed to his proposed budget cuts. Other special interest groups sympathetic to some of his objectives rallied to his support and were a major factor in the success of his effort.

A special interest group can be a strong foe, a powerful ally or, most distressingly if unnoticed, a potential political "land mine." By understanding the road map of organized special interest groups and systematically creating appropriate tactics to use or mitigate their influences, strategic processes can make a vital contribution to effective government management.

The Decline of Political Parties

Political parties have lost much of their influence in American society and American politics. They no longer have sole power to determine policies, secure legislation or implement programs. As the importance of political parties has diminished, the committee structures of the Congress and many state legislatures have abandoned seniority systems and emasculated the powers of committee chairmen, further weakening the party structure.

Consequently, many campaigning politicians correctly argue that they are literally on their own and can fly political "flags of convenience." The "boll weevil" and "gypsy moth" movements in Congress in 1981–82, in which Members of the Congress openly broke party ranks in large numbers, would have been unthinkable as late as the 1960s.

Today, many officials are being elected without fully developing their platforms, a fundamental service previously provided by the party. As a result, newly elected officials often find themselves in office with proposed programs, ideas and themes that require enormous refinement before being sent to the legislative branch. This trend helps explain the recent popularity of blue ribbon commissions in attempts not only to create coalitions, but also to find solutions.

The fact that a majority of the legislative body belongs to the same party as the Chief Elected Official no longer guarantees the passage or implementation of a particular policy or program. With the decline of party influence, elected officials must often transcend party lines and party mechanisms to build the political coalitions necessary to effect all or part of a strategy. Under these circumstances, political coalitions and opposition organized along party lines are difficult to construct and maintain. Indeed, the coalition required to implement one part of a program may be different from that required for other parts. And political success or failure often hinges on an effective understanding of these distinctions. And it can be done. Governor Winter of Mississippi, for example, has successfully constructed a political coalition to reform that state's education programs.

Inherent in the strategic management of government is the orderly construction of coalitions, even shifting coalitions over time, to implement the many facets of an administration's overall program. Clearly, a strategic approach is part of the answer to filling the political vacuum created by the decline of America's political parties.

Intergovernmental Competition

Competition is the hallmark of American federalism. In the absence of shared objectives and strategies, this competition often becomes destructive, wasting scarce resources and limiting the effectiveness of whatever public programs are mounted. The consequent policy and program fragmentation produces the following problems:

- policies, programs and resources are splintered among and between levels of government;
- procedures conflict because of different funding cycles, planning requirements, eligibility standards, political objectives and administrative processes;
- program delivery systems vary widely, even within the same functional areas, thus building bulwarks against focused action; and
- authorities do not match responsibilities.

In turn, numerous policy and management perversions are created—a loss of accountability among elected and appointed officials; limited pooling of public resources; the duplication of some services and omission of others—while public frustration and cynicism about government mount.

Although the nation cannot afford such waste and confusion, reorganizations and shifts of authorities and responsibilities within the federalist system have failed to correct these deficiencies. As a result, political nihilism is flourishing. Elected officials are running against the very governments they were elected to manage and, in the process, creating management programs that eliminate entire functions of government.

Fortunately, it is not necessary to overhaul American federalism to create better management in American government. The processes of strategic vision and management offer a pragmatic and effective alternative.

If the destructive effects of intergovernmental competition are to be overcome, the federal government and affected state and local governments will have to agree first on specific goals and then on strategies to achieve them. Many techniques for reaching such an agreement are available.

One of the more intriguing of these techniques has been developed by the Charles F. Kettering Foundation. It has assisted a number of state and local governments in developing such strategies and agreements through a process known as the Negotiated Investment Strategy (NIS). A formal bargaining process brings together a neutral mediator with representatives of the federal, state and local governments. The NIS process attempts to coordinate policies, programs and available resources at each level of government to meet jointly determined objectives. The NIS process has shown real progress in improving government management in Gary, Indiana; St. Paul, Minnesota; and Columbus, Ohio. The State of Connecticut has been successful in using the NIS process to negotiate the use of social service block grants with local governments and social service providers.

Other techniques are also available. The point is that massive reorganization of government, or federalism, is not needed to improve the management of government.

Separation of Powers

Just as American federalism was designed to ensure creative tension between the levels of government, the separation of powers between the legislative, judicial and executive branches guarantees another form of competition. The flow of power between the executive and legislative branches is dynamic, reflecting particular circumstances and the force of personalities. Similarly, there is often intense competition among and between the executive and legislative branches as agencies and committees battle for turf. Managing this competition is essential to the effective management of government.

During the past 20 years, the legislative branches of virtually every level of government have expanded their capacities and influence through increased staff and technical support and a variety of legislative oversight powers. In many states and at the federal and local levels as well, long-standing political feuds, staff inexperience, conflicting time perspectives and opposing constituents work to undermine the potential for cooperation. In a few states, competition between the governor and legislature has escalated to where new approaches are essential if there is to be any shared strategic vision of the state's long-term direction.

Fortunately, a Chief Elected Official can moderate nonpartisan—and sometimes even partisan—dimensions of competition by simply reaching some agreement on basic circumstances, negotiating a set of clear objectives and then permitting the joint political "ownership" of these objectives with the legislative body.

The Media

The media frequently becomes a scapegoat for governmental mismanagement. In part this is because the media controls the principal means of communication between government and the voters. And the filter on the media's vision is often negative since journalists still advance their careers by reporting scandals, failure and the ever present internecine warfare among political leaders.

Yet the media is also a translator, educator and advocate of government policies and a supporter or detractor of individual officials. Just as no campaign is complete without a media strategy, government management strategies are incomplete, or at least highly vulnerable, without a clear media plan. Strategic vision and management techniques can be used to create a comprehensive communication strategy that can help explain policies and respond to inevitable criticism.

In sum, politics are a reality of management. By recognizing that reality and managing the politics the CEO better assures the success of the institution's goals, plans and operations. Systematic foresight, goal setting, and strategic planning help in that management process. However if that process is to be systematic, a framework for analysis and action is required.

CHAPTER 3

A Framework

CHIEF ELECTED OFFICIALS and their top managers should not expect easy or quick solutions to the ongoing, deeply rooted deficiencies in government management. Improvements will require strong, interrelated measures taken over time as specific needs are broadly perceived and understood. At their core, these actions must be based on a: (a) systematic analysis of pivotal long-term trends and issues—economic, technological, demographic, political, social and international—that are likely to influence the environment in which the institution will operate; and (b) comprehensive analysis of the institution's capacity to respond to those trends. On the basis of these analyses, the institution can explicitly identify its fundamental objectives and how to achieve them.

If these and other elements of a strategic management process are to fit into an ordered whole, a framework is required for the many separate decisions and actions that will shape both short- and long-range results. Such a strategic management framework for issues identification, goal setting, planning, decision-making and implementation has four important advantages for public CEOs: first, it can help government officials identify, classify and explicitly consider seemingly unrelated government decisions; second, it can be used to assess the many direct and indirect consequences of those decisions; third, it can be used to structure an implementation strategy that draws on all available political and management resources and tools; and finally, it permits improved day-to-day operational management without massive governmental streamlining and reorganization.

An effective framework for strategic management, applicable to both public and private sectors, consists of five interrelated components:

1. *Foresight*—explicit efforts to systematically identify, monitor and analyze long-term trends and issues likely to affect the institution's future environment and to examine the implications of those trends on various actions the institution might take;

2. *Goal Setting*—the explicit definition of the basic aims of the institution;

3. *Strategic Planning*—the process of identifying the resources to be used in attaining those aims and the policies that are to govern the acquisition, use and disposition of those resources;

4. *Operational Management*—the translation of goals and strategies into ongoing operations; and

5. *Evaluation*—the systematic review of the goals, strategies and operations of the institution, along with the preparation of recommendations for needed adjustments.

All of these parts of the whole are interconnected. Each involves different actions, and each is important (see Figures 1 and 2).

Unfortunately, any discussion of strategic concepts is hampered by the imprecision of the terminology, the virtual absence of common terms and definitions. Foresight activity, for example, is also known as issues management, emerging issues analysis and futures research. Such semantic confusion is perhaps characteristic of a discipline that is an art and not a science. (See Appendix B for a lexicon of commonly used terms.)

For analytical purposes, a useful distinction can be drawn between strategic and operational management functions. Generally, strategic functions are those associated with foresight, goal setting and strategic planning. Thus, they include the analysis of the institution's present and prospective environment(s), the selection of goals, the identification of resources to meet those goals, and the formulation of basic policies to guide the acquisition and use of those resources. Strategic decisions will determine the fundamental, longer term purposes and directions of the institution. In government, the process of identifying or redefining institutional objectives usually coincides with a change of political administration or the beginning of a second term.

Strategic thinking involves assessing the "futurity" of decisions: the future consequences on the organization of either long- or short-term decisions that fundamentally affect the organization's goals. Strategic decisions that have long-term effects on a company are often made in response to short-term opportunities or events, such as the purchase of another company that may unexpectedly be for sale.

Operational functions are those associated with operational management and evaluation. They are designed to as-

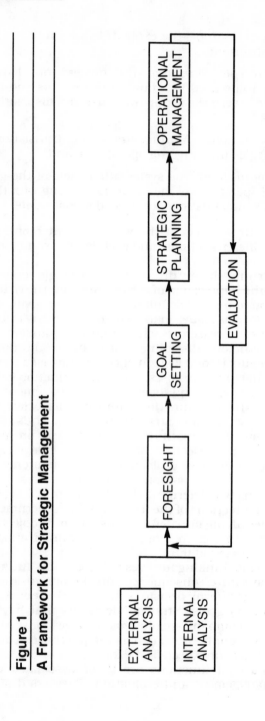

Figure 1

A Framework for Strategic Management

sure that resources are obtained and then effectively and efficiently used to achieve strategic objectives. Operational management involves activities such as deciding on routine actions and expenditures; determining staff levels; developing better ways to implement projects; formulating liaison and coordination programs; selecting research projects; ensuring that policies are actually implemented in the activities and programs of the organization; formulating personnel policies, program and operating budgets, and allocations; and formulating and implementing an evaluation system.

Most operational management activities are cyclical—that is, they follow a definite pattern and timetable that is repeated. In budgeting, for example, certain steps will be taken in a prescribed sequence and by prescribed dates. Original budget estimates are prepared, estimates are reviewed, approval is given and then final decisions are disseminated through the organization. The procedures to be followed at each step, such as deadlines and even the forms to be used, are specified for each cycle of this recurring process.[12]

In most corporations, the distinction between operational and strategic decisions is embodied in the division of responsibilities between the President and Chief Executive Officer: the president is usually the Chief *Operating* Officer whose primary responsibility is operational management, while the CEO concentrates on strategic decisions.

Interactions between strategic and operational management are intricate, however, and the line between the two is often blurred. But in the final analysis, operational management involves activities that implement a strategy within guidelines established in the strategic planning process. For example, a company's decision to enter a new field of business is a strategic decision. The day-to-day decisions involved in running that business are operational. Similarly, a state's decision to create a state bond bank is a strategic decision. But the local bonds it selects to finance in a given year is an operational decision.

The key components of strategic vision and management represent a continuum of strategic activities. However, it is the foresight function that is giving new life to strategic thinking and action. Corporations have always engaged in some form of long-range planning. It was not until the early 1970s that "strategic" planning became popular in many large corporations. Yet by the late 1970s, while some companies were abandoning strategic planning because of its narrow focus and disappointing results, others were introducing a new function—foresight— that not only enhanced the effectiveness of strategic planning,

Figure 2
Key Elements of Strategic Management in Government

Foresight	Goal Setting	Strategic Planning	Operational Management	Evaluation/Feedback
Identify basic trends and pivotal events—internal and external to the institution.	Identify the need for action and the ability to influence; then establish the institution's priorities.	Choose objectives (policy, program, and political).	Formulate and implement rules for controlling and managing the organization.	
		Structure the organization (formal and informal).	Create/modify organizational structure.	
		Set personnel, appointment, and patronage policies.	Plan the staff levels—create and implement personnel practices.	
		Establish finance policy (tax, user fees and other revenue options).	Create and implement budgets.	
		Establish expenditure/regulatory policies, including evaluation/feedback policies.	Decide on and take program decisions/actions. Create an evaluation/feedback system.	
		Establish information, liaison, and coordination policies.	Create and implement information, liaison, and coordination programs.	
		Set research policies.	Choose and conduct research projects.	
		Establish a legislative strategy.	Implement the legislative strategy.	
		Set policies for non-routine events and expenditures.		
		Set the political strategy (timing, referendum and initiative, fundraisers, party leadership, and intergovernmental politics).	Create a political agenda (priorities, timetable, lobbying, deal-making).	

but also organized and gave new direction to those companies overall strategic activities. In essence, the information gained from the foresight process enabled companies to develop the *strategic vision* needed to guide and support their goal-setting, planning and operational activities.

Foresight, therefore, is the cutting edge of the entire strategic process. With foresight, clear goals and strategic plans can be constructed and linked to operations. In both business and government, efforts to improve the quality of management have failed repeatedly when they have focused on day-to-day operational management that was not linked to foresight, clear goals, and an overall strategic plan.

Foresight

Numerous trends and events affect the management of business and government. The nuclear freeze movement, oil embargoes, the environmental movement, Proposition 13 and other tax-cutting measures, demographic changes, and the decline of the nation's education system are only the most visible examples of trends and events that have important, if not fundamental, influences on the decisions and actions of business and government alike. The earlier these trends and events can be identified, the wider the range of options the CEO and the institution (public or private) will have.

Today and for the foreseeable future, successful management of the public sector, as in the private sector, requires the systematic identification and analysis of these trends and events. Then realistic goals can be set, specific strategies can be created, and programs can be managed effectively.

A number of major corporations and governmental organizations have recognized the benefits of the early anticipation of events and trends. A partial listing of the organizations that have created foresight units includes Sears, Allstate, General Electric, TRW, Upjohn, Prudential, Atlantic Richfield, 3M, Monsanto, General Motors, Security Pacific National Bank, Dupont, Westinghouse, McDonald's, the General Accounting Office, the State of Ohio, the National Bureau of Standards, and the Army Materiel Development and Readiness Command.

As documented in a survey by the National Science Foundation (NSF), the foresight units in these organizations explicitly engage in activities to determine "important social, economic, political, educational, scientific, or technological changes" that will affect the operations of the organizations.[13]

The NSF also found that in most organizations foresight activities were "both systematic and continual, as well as specialized and reactive to specific requirements, and served broad, overall strategic planning as well as operational purposes." The survey also found that:

- Organizations have different geographic concerns, ranging from a single country and its regions (generally the United States) to groups of countries and sometimes to the world.
- The time horizon for foresight activities varied considerably: one to two years for operational issues; three to five years for specific issues; and five to ten years or longer for long-term planning.
- Business planning tended to be more long-term, sometimes up to 20 years or more; however, the federal government's planning was more short-term, reflecting the one- to three-year budget cycle and preoccupation with immediate pressures, such as those created by the Congress.

Most important, the survey found that when armed with a realistic assessment of how a particular trend or issue was likely to affect its operations, these organizations would alter their goals (even completely redefine them), creating a new strategic vision in the process. Sears, for example, developed a new strategic vision based on analyses that suggested only limited growth in future retail sales but virtually unlimited growth potential in consumer financial services.

At the federal level, several organizations engage in some foresight activities. For example, the Committee on Energy and Commerce of the House of Representatives (now defunct) established a Congressional Foresight Network. Drawn from the public and private sectors, this network was established to assist the Committee in identifying pivotal issues, assessing their consequences and proposing alternative responses. The Congressional Clearinghouse on the Future, formed in 1976, is a coalition of more than 100 Senators and Representatives who attend monthly meetings with analysts to review and discuss long-term issues and trends. The Clearinghouse has an in-house Trend Identification and Monitoring program which provides an early warning service for Congress.

Selected foresight activities are also conducted by the Congressional support agencies—the Congressional Budget Office, General Accounting Office, Office of Technology Assessment and Congressional Research Service. The Congressional Research Service also assists congressional staff in futures research and develops futures information and forecasts of value to Members of the Congress.

The National Science Foundation prepares the *Five-Year Outlook in Science and Technology.* And the Bureau of Land Management, the Central Intelligence Agency (CIA), Forest Service and parts of the Department of Transportation conduct futures activities as well.

Since 1970, more than 25 states have engaged in some kind of foresight activity. Foresight units in the state governments of Utah and Kansas are responsible for identifying and analyzing pivotal issues and trends that will affect these state governments. New York has established a Council for Economic Alternatives to advise the Governor on economic trends and possible responses. North Carolina has recently concluded a massive effort entitled *North Carolina 2000* which identifies local and area views of what the state's future should be and the actions required to realize that future.

Thus, in both the public and private sectors, effective foresight is coming to be recognized as an integral part of the strategic management process. Decisions, after all, are no better than the quality of thought and information on which they are based. And the better that information is and the earlier it can be obtained, the more proactive goals, strategies and programs can be.

Two kinds of analyses dominate foresight work: external analysis and internal analysis. The *external analysis* of an organization's future environment includes what is known as emerging issues analysis, forecasting and scenario development. The growing body of literature about issues identification and analysis demonstrates the wide variations in techniques and organizational approaches that companies are using in this process. Some engage specialized consulting firms that follow issues, while others employ staff who systematically identify key trends by conducting issue analysis themselves and by monitoring the activities and publications of other groups engaged in issues analysis. (See Appendix C for a brief description of the various foresight techniques now being used by businesses and governments).

Whatever techniques are used, foresight work provides information about specific opportunities and threats that the company or government must address in its strategic planning and operations. One important benefit of this process is that it forces an organization to give the same attention to future events and trends as it traditionally gives to near-term issues and problems.

Although some organizations in both the public and private sectors have been reluctant to undertake futures analyses because of a perceived lack of data, the necessary information is indeed available. If anything, there is too much data. Since so much of the existing information is fragmented, however, the real challenge is to organize it in a meaningful way.

The importance of issues analysis for a public entity is demonstrated by the continuing impact of immigration on the State of Florida. For example, what conditions in Cuba contributed to its decision to permit, even facilitate, the mass exodus of Cubans to Florida in 1980? Could these conditions have been anticipated? Could they recur and, if so, what should this nation's response be? What should be the response of the State of Florida?

A few states have programs that monitor demographic and economic information. *Texas Trends,* published by the *Texas 2000* project, is a recent example.[14] *Choices for Pennsylvania* represents another major effort to examine trends and directions at the state level.[15] Several other states have also prepared reports on critical issues. The Illinois Bureau of the Budget has produced a report, "The Baby Boom Generation: Impacts on State Revenues and Spending, 1950–2025," which analyzes the effects of one of the most predictable trends.[16] The State of Ohio has prepared an analysis of Ohio's economy which identifies pivotal forces affecting that economy (now and in the future), alternative actions that could be taken, and a proposed state economic strategy.[17] Together, these efforts demonstrate a clear understanding by some leading governors of the need for external analyses and how to apply them.

Internal analysis is used to evaluate an institution's capacity to respond to events or issues identified in the external analysis. Using the Cuban immigration example again, the State of Florida conducted an internal analysis to assess its capacity to assume the welfare responsibility for arriving Cubans. The analysis documented in advance that the state did not have the resources to handle the problem without substantial federal assistance.

As part of doing business, private firms systematically identify the likely course of events, as well as changes in company policy that might be required to adjust to changing realities. These internal analyses assess the organization's capacity to respond to change and capture the opportunities that change presents. If there are weaknesses in a company's ability to respond effectively to anticipated events and trends, then the internal analysis identifies the options, costs and actions required to overcome them.

Goal Setting

If foresight information is to be integrated effectively into the operations of an organization, it must be systematically considered in the organization's goal-setting and decision-making processes.

A number of businesses use "strategic matrices" as a decision-making framework for identifying issues and creating priorities for action. There are substantial variations in the strategic matrix techniques developed by firms such as the Boston Consulting Group, Strategic Planning Associates, McKinsey and Associates, Arthur D. Little and Company, General Electric and others. Essentially, however, these matrices enable senior executives to relate a company's strengths (such as current market share) to industry or product attractiveness (as indicated, for example, in its potential profits and growth). A recent *Fortune* article noted that by 1981, half the Fortune 1,000 industrial corporations were using some type of growth-share matrix in their planning.

Figure 3 illustrates in simplified form how these matrices permit firms to consider their internal strengths and weaknesses (*ability to influence*) as they relate to specific industries or products (*need for action*). The nine-cell matrix is a conceptual device that enables firms to define high-, medium- and low-priority actions. In the process, this technique helps organize information, and focus discussion and policymaking.

The organizing and priority-setting technique embodied in the strategic matrix concept is equally applicable to government, with only slight modification. Specifically:

- For business, the *need for action* is defined by factors such as market potential, possible profitability and potential vulnerabilities. For government, in contrast, the need for action is defined by other factors such as constitutional mandates, election promises and political pressures.

- For business, the *ability to influence* decisions and actions is defined by factors such as company size, available capital, quality of management and workers, market share and technological positions. For government, the ability to influence decisions and actions is defined by factors such as

Figure 3
The Nine-Cell Decision Matrix

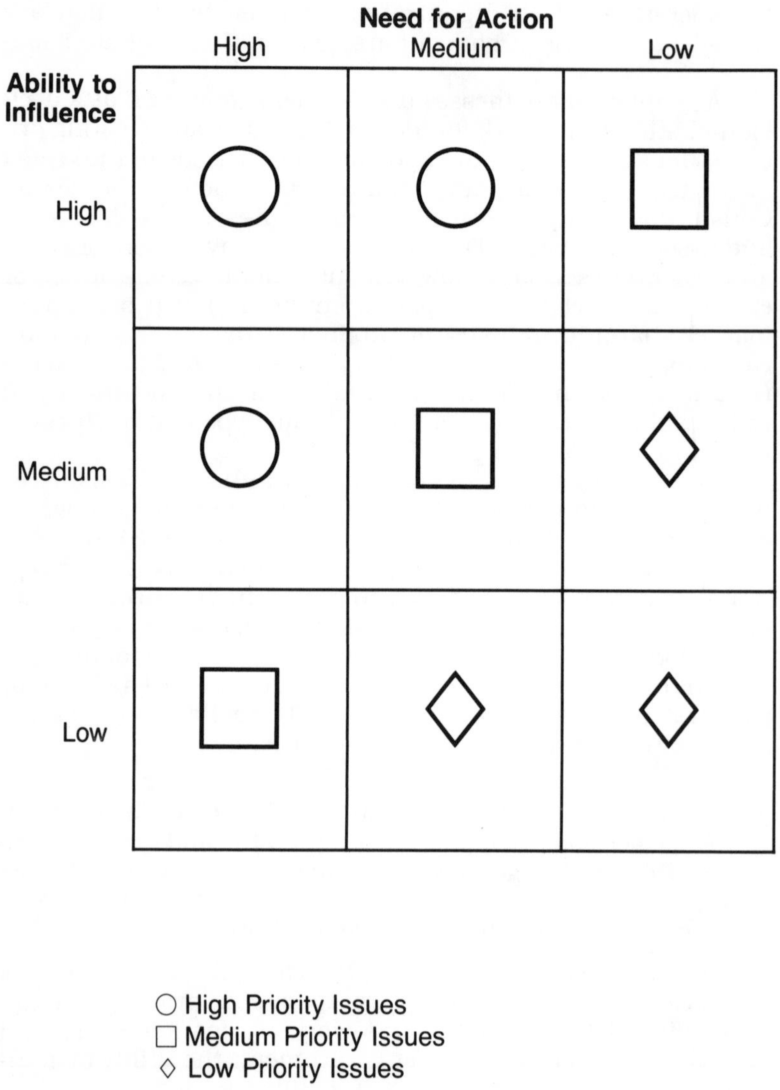

Need for Action

Ability to Influence	High	Medium	Low
High	◯	◯	☐
Medium	◯	☐	◇
Low	☐	◇	◇

◯ High Priority Issues
☐ Medium Priority Issues
◇ Low Priority Issues

public opinion, legislation, executive control, fiscal capacities and constitutions.

Assessments of the need for action and the ability to influence actions and decisions are therefore central to the formulation of effective strategies in both the public and private sectors. Strategic goal setting in any organization, then, is a three-step process:

1. the need for action must be evaluated;

2. the organization's ability to influence actions and decisions must be assessed; and

3. the need for an organization to act must be compared with its ability to act and influence decisions.

A public-sector CEO must analyze a wide range of issues to determine the need and ability to take action. First, however, it is necessary to identify the basic areas in which issues may arise and decisions may have to be taken—issues and decisions that will often compete for the same resources and attention. These areas would likely include economic policy, social services, recreation, natural resources/environment, agriculture, foreign policy, defense, public safety, capital improvements, education and training, and research and development.

Obviously, the range of areas that are pertinent to an elected official will vary among levels of government and in the context of specific circumstances. For example, both the President and a governor would have decision-making responsibilities for transportation, but a governor does not for foreign policy.

The factors that influence the need for action require detailed specification. Constitutional, statutory, regulatory and court-mandated responsibilities could all affect a governor's ability to act. The need for action could also be influenced by discretionary responsibilities such as campaign promises, party platforms, constituency needs, personal values and the nature of the issue itself (see Figure 4).

In any circumstance, the combination of these factors will alter the need for action. In some states, for example, a campaign promise to create more and better jobs may mean that economic policy is a high priority. In another state, a deteriorating environment and federal mandates may raise the environmental issue to the top of a governor's agenda. The point is that each governor, mayor or other public official, including the President, will have different priorities. For each unit of govern-

Figure 4

The Need for Action

Factors	Policy Areas			
	Economic Policy	Social Services	Recreation	Environment/ Resources
Mandated Responsibilities				
constitutional				
statutory				
rules				
court-ordered				
Discretionary Responsibilities				
campaign promises				
party platforms				
constituency				
nature of the issues				
quality-of-life				
efficiency				
equity				
life/death				
Personal Values				
Other				

INSTRUCTIONS

In rank ordering by importance, use a scale of 3, 2, 1, 0, or X. The shading of meanings are as follows:

3 — critical and must be addressed.
2 — important and merits attention.
1 — a low priority.
0 — unimportant.
X — do not know.

Policy Areas						
Agriculture	Foreign	Defense	Public Safety	Capital	Education	Research/ Development

ment, moreover, these priorities will vary over time. The benefit of strategic management in this process is that it provides a systematic approach and explicit criteria for identifying responsibilities and needs and then for setting priorities.

After the need for action has been clearly established, the ability to influence decisions and actions must be assessed. Factors that determine the ability to influence actions include political circumstances, institutional relationships, fiscal and other resources, and the managerial and staff capacities to take action (see Figure 5). Here again, in each situation, a combination of these factors will influence a public leader's response. In this step of the process as well, the value of strategic management is its systematic approach and use of precise criteria to set priorities.

Strategy

This methodical approach to priority setting is much like the strategic matrix approach used by many companies. After the need/ability assessments have been completed, the need for government action must be measured against its ability to act and influence decisions. It makes no sense, after all, to address an issue that is of little importance or, conversely, one whose outcome the public CEO has little ability to influence.

A governor in a state served by the Tennessee Valley Authority (TVA), for example, might want to influence decisions concerning the operation of a nuclear generating plant. Since the TVA is an autonomous federal agency, however, the governor's ability to influence those decisions may be quite low. In setting goals and priorities, therefore, the governor might choose to focus resources, time and attention in an area such as state highway construction, education or worker training, where the demand for state action and the state's ability to influence decisions both run strong.

Because resources—time, political strength, people and money—are always limited, choices must be made. In the public sector, this means that a President, governor or mayor must narrow his or her agenda to a few issues that are both important and possible to influence. The attention devoted to other issues will focus primarily on the effective management of ongoing policies and programs.

This entire goal-setting process has many important advantages. In his book, *Top Management Planning*, George A.

Steiner identifies five significant benefits of systematic goal setting which apply *equally* to the public and private sectors:

1. The existence of specific goals and the participation of people in establishing them have great motivational power.

2. Goals guide the actions and decisions of managers.

3. They set the basic philosophy or tone of an organization.

4. They help establish and improve an organization's image.

5. They provide a basis for analyzing and evaluating performance.[18]

Thus, the systematic identification of pivotal issues and events and subsequent use of a systematic goal-setting process enhance the CEO's ability to perform a CEO's most important functions—setting the goals of the institution, determining priorities, and establishing the basic policies that will guide the acquisition and use of resources to meet specific goals.

This approach can be extremely effective in the public sector. Governors Jay S. Hammond of Alaska and Richard L. Thornburgh of Pennsylvania have used it to make state policy and resource allocations. Before the budget cycle begins each year, they issue short, easy-to-understand policy directives and general strategies to be used in agency budget preparation. Agency budget requests and planned activities are then reviewed for their consistency with the outlined goals.

Naturally, an elected official's goals and strategies will include some issues and actions not directly related to management of the government bureaucracy—that is, political goals that do not depend on bureaucratic achievements. For example, former Governor Reubin Askew of Florida was able to parlay success in statewide referenda on nonbureaucratic issues, such as full financial disclosure for public officials and opposition to casino gambling, into increased overall influence with the bureaucracy and legislature.

Strategy is the plan for achieving specific goals. In the private sector, the strategic plan integrates questions such as what business the company should be in, where to invest, what products to offer, where to produce and what markets to enter. Although public-sector strategy questions are vastly different, the same logic applies. Public CEOs need overall plans to integrate investment, resource and program decisions into a unified approach. In place of the price, advertising and trade policies that constitute business strategy, considerations such

Figure 5

The Ability to Influence

Factors	Policy Areas			
	Economic Policy	Social Services	Recreation	Environment/ Resources
Political Factors				
public opinion				
political fund raising				
legislative				
political party				
special interests				
press				
opinion leaders				
personalities				
public interest/ issue groups				
Institutional Factors				
businesses				
academics				
labor				
quasi-public groups				
policy institutes				
associations				
caucuses				
public/private organizations				
Intergovernmental Factors				
federal				
multi-state				
state				
areawide				
local				
Economic Factors				
financial capacity				
state of the economy				
Managerial Factors				
quality of staff				
quantity of staff				
logistical support				
Other				

INSTRUCTIONS

In rank ordering by importance, use a scale of 3, 2, 1, 0, or X. The shading of meanings are as follows:

Policy Areas						
Agriculture	Foreign	Defense	Public Safety	Capital	Education	Research/ Development

3 — critical and must be addressed.
2 — important and merits attention.
1 — a low priority.
0 — unimportant.
X — do not know.

as taxation, public expenditures and regulatory policy comprise government strategy. To create and advance an integrated strategy, public officials can use a variety of tools, including the following:

1. the budget;
2. the legislative program;
3. executive orders;
4. reorganization;
5. appointments;
6. press relations;
7. cabinet meetings;
8. private-sector liaison;
9. relations with interest groups; and
10. the conduct of government programs.

Clearly, the opportunities and tools are available to public-sector CEOs to define goals sharply and systematically and then to create effective strategies: the challenge is to use these opportunities effectively. A strategic approach provides a systematic and explicit means of successfully meeting this challenge.

CHAPTER 4

Creating and Implementing A Strategic Vision

COMMON SENSE DOMINATES strategic thinking. That is why the public and private organizations that have successfully applied strategic approaches have done so with divergent procedures and techniques. Each has tailored the concepts of foresight, goal setting and strategic planning to the organization's own circumstances, needs, culture, even to the personalities of those involved. Despite these individual differences, however, organizations with successful strategic processes share a number of striking characteristics:

- The CEO and top management are committed to strategic processes.
- The institutions are organized either formally or informally for strategic management, and foresight and strategic planning activities are a normal part of the management of the institution. Since strategic management techniques are tailor made to each institution, the organizational structure for strategic management differs, often significantly, between organizations.
- The institutions give explicit attention to creating and nurturing a *culture* of strategic management. And the most vital catalyst for creating and nurturing this culture is the full support and participation of the Chief Executive Officer or Chief Elected Official.
- The organizations use a strategic planning and policy cycle that usually precedes, but always includes, the budget cycle.
- Time and resources are devoted to defining, understanding and reassessing the major missions and goals of the organization and to developing long- and short-term policies and actions to achieve those goals.
- The systematic analysis of the institution's environment and its internal capacities to respond to that environment are part of the strategic planning process.

- Clear relationships between policies, resources and the strategic plans are established to meet institutional objectives.
- Choices are presented in a manner that clearly shows the spectrum of available alternatives, their costs and their consequences.
- Each aspect of the organization's performance is measured against plans; such performance evaluation serves as the foundation for creating and extending organizational and personal incentives.
- Managers are trained to use a broad range of strategic management concepts and techniques.

Creating a strategic vision for an organization and then translating it into strategic plans and operations often require difficult adjustments in attitudes, behavior patterns and expectations. The difficulties of implementation will be minimized, however, if top-level managers are committed to the process and line managers are convinced of its value at the very outset. The concept should not be oversold; nor should the time demands, frustrations and costs associated with the new initiative be understated.

Commitment to strategic processes will not be enough, however. Decisions and actions must be taken on a number of important factors, including the organizational structure that will be used; the size and role of the planning staff; establishment of a planning calendar; allocation of resources; creation of evaluation procedures; and how the organization's culture can be adapted to support the entire strategic process.

The Commitment of Top Management

Because permanent and substantive change is so difficult to achieve in any organization, the introduction of foresight and strategic planning processes requires the expressed and continuing commitment of top officials. Since responsibility for the creation of a strategic vision and its translation into a strategic plan resides with the CEO, the CEO and other principal executives must have a clear understanding of the logic, costs, benefits, advantages and disadvantages of what is to be done. Equally important, they must be able to articulate that understanding to others both inside and outside the organization.

George Steiner summarizes top management's role in such a process as follows:

- Without the CEO's support, participation and guidance, the process will fail.
- Vision and planning are ultimately the responsibility of the CEO and cannot be delegated to a planning staff.
- The CEO is responsible for assuring that a proper organization for the process is created, that the manner of its functioning is clear and understood, and that it operates effectively and efficiently.
- The CEO must make certain that all managers understand that planning is a continuous function and not one pursued on an ad hoc basis or only during a formal planning cycle.
- Once plans are prepared, top management must make decisions on the basis of those plans.[19]

The CEO's support and commitment are especially critical during the implementation phases. Virtually every corporation that has instituted strategic planning has encountered resistance from its managers at the outset—resistance that generally dissipates as managers gain experience using systematic strategic processes and techniques.

For example, a survey of operating managers at General Electric found that after many years of experience with strategic processes, they were "so comfortable with strategic planning and so convinced of its benefits that they would continue to do it even if not required as a company management process." The kind of enthusiasm demonstrated at GE can be expected only after many years of steadfast commitment by top management.

This kind of commitment is also possible in the public sector. Governors Richard A. Snelling of Vermont and Scott M. Matheson of Utah have created foresight and strategic planning processes that are a regular part of state management. Governor Snelling, for instance, requires all agency heads to detail how their proposed actions and use of resources will help meet the specific goals that guide his Administration.

How the processes of foresight, goal setting and strategic planning will be designed and linked to ongoing operations must, as with any management improvement, be tailored to the structure, political culture and history of the organization. Top management will have to decide, for example, whether the effort should be announced publicly or treated as a quiet internal management initiative.

Regardless of what design is adopted, "planning productivity" should be emphasized to avert a backlash against
"additional bureaucratic requirements from top management.
Planning productivity can be enhanced by focusing only on key
issues, increasing the quality of analyses, and limiting the time
required for planning by managers. This is absolutely essential
because line managers in the public sector contend daily with
demanding responsibilities, such as managing state mental
hospitals or administering hazardous waste programs, that
claim much of their attention and personal energy.

Gaining their support for the systematic creation and implementation of a strategic vision will require five important
steps:

1. An effective explanation of the *evolutionary* nature of
the process.

2. The creation of managerial task forces to adapt the generic principles of foresight, goal setting and strategic planning to fit the organization. The support of these managers will
be needed in the implementation phases.

3. Demonstrations of the process and system in a limited
area of the organization to develop support and experience and
to give an early taste of success.

4. Anticipation of the predictable swings of enthusiasm
and even rejection during the first planning cycle, so initial
disappointments can be minimized.

5. A substantial investment in training line managers in
strategic concepts.

The provision of adequate training for the line managers
who will be charged with implementing the plans is crucial to
the success of a strategic approach. For example, before General Electric launched its first strategic planning effort, the
company made a serious commitment to training its management force. Specifically, 320 top executives received four days of
off-site orientation; 428 planners attended a two-week strategic
planning workshop; and 10,000 managers received one day of
awareness training.

Because foresight, goal setting and strategic planning cannot be carried out by a hastily recruited cadre of central planners, implementation must be geared to convincing and
developing an organization's managers. These managers must
produce most of the required information and analyses for this
effort and must learn to think and operate within the logic of

the strategic approach as well. Task forces, demonstrations and training are therefore essential—not only to gain the support of line managers, but also to foster a sense of ownership of the new management initiative.

With these two requisites in place—the commitment of top-level management and support of line managers—an organization is ready to begin to think, plan and operate strategically.

Organization

In both the private and public sectors, a variety of organizational configurations have been used successfully for foresight and strategic planning. Indeed, there are as many models for organizational structures, procedures and channels of communication as there are organizations. The National Science Foundation survey on foresight found that the foresight function was usually most successful when organized to use the professional skills available in each of several groups—groups engaged, for example, in strategic planning or policy analysis, issues scanning or ongoing management. Thus, a principal advantage of a strategic approach, particularly for government leaders, is that it is not constrained by organizational charts, but instead can draw from any group, program or agency to address a major goal.

Many companies organize their strategic activities around distinct planning and administrative units called Strategic Business Units (SBUs). An SBU is a business unit that sells a product or group of related products to a definable market and has identifiable competitors in that market. An SBU may be any size and can be located at any level of the organization.

The federal government and several states, such as Massachusetts, use a similar technique known as the "cabinet council" approach. Using this technique, several distinct agencies or programs that have responsibilities in a particular area, such as economic development or education, are brought together for planning and administrative purposes.

An approach based on "strategic units" allows the top manager—the President, governor, mayor or agency head—to emphasize priority programs, devise common goals, formulate a strategic plan and focus operations *without reorganizing*. It also permits managers to focus both staff and financial resources on key program areas without initiating a government-wide or agency-wide program. In short, the use of flexible strategic units minimizes the importance of organizational structure by providing a way to concentrate directly on needed programs and actions.

Staff

Responsibility for developing and facilitating the foresight, goal-setting and strategic planning processes is usually assigned to a staff. Yet only a small staff is required when expertise throughout the company or government is used to deal with specific issues. The staff creates a process for identifying and analyzing major issues, brings that information to the attention of goal setters and assures that the strategic planning process proceeds according to the planning calendar, which it also establishes. As with all key staff functions, the effectiveness of this staff hinges not only on its competence, but also on its access to the Chief Elected/Executive Officer.

In many organizations, this staff reports directly to the CEO. But in other organizations, the staff that facilitates strategic activity is found in departments, divisions, branches or other offices. In several major companies, senior line and staff officers provide assistance to those engaged in foresight and strategic planning, often through formal issues management or public policy committees.

The staff that is charged with foresight and strategic planning activities often has a wide range of responsibilities, which typically include the following:

- working with the CEO to create the foresight and planning process, assisting in the development of long-range goals and strategies to meet them;
- undertaking special studies requested by top management;
- scanning the organization's environment including key economic, social, political and technological trends;
- analyzing the organization's ability to respond to important changes in its external environment;
- coordinating and reviewing plans for efficiency and consistency;
- providing departments and agencies with technical assistance, including both procedural and substantive guidance such as forecasts of environmental factors relevant to a particular planning activity;
- developing alternative plans for the CEO's consideration; and
- assisting in implementation activities, when requested.

Clearly, the specific roles and duties of this staff depend on the personality of the CEO and the size and nature of the organization. Some of these planning functions, as well as the staff resources, are already in place in most governments, often in the mayor's, governor's or President's office.

The Planning Calendar

Implementation of the entire strategic management process—foresight, goal setting, strategic planning, operational management and evaluation—requires a planning calendar. By systematically considering its present and prospective operating environment, along with its goals, strategies and programs, an organization can better link the separate elements of its strategic management process.

Once a planning schedule is established, it must be followed closely. Virtually every major corporation engaged in strategic planning has a fixed planning cycle. As part of that cycle, line and staff departments generally maintain five-year plans and one-year plans. The five-year plan is updated annually to ensure that the company's longer term strategic vision is always considered. Simultaneously, the one-year plan details what actions will be taken in the short term to fulfill that longer term vision.

As part of this process, many corporations conduct off-site sessions to review performance and test the basic assumptions that will guide the preparation of their longer and shorter term plans. Good foresight is particularly important at this stage when goals and assumptions are being tested, reviewed and adopted. The high priority assigned to these sessions is evident in the extent of top-level participation: the meetings are led by the CEO and attended by most senior executives.

For the public sector, there are at least three important advantages in developing and using a planning calendar:

- Short-term budgeting becomes secondary to the identification of basic goals, the creation of strategies to meet them, and the establishment of a framework in which resources can be allocated. Thus, budgeting is no longer viewed as an independent process in and of itself, but rather as an integral part of a thoughtful strategic process.
- Managerial participation is assured.
- CEOs are able to consider systematically the viewpoints of key managers.

The value of a planning calendar in the public sector has been demonstrated in the State of Utah. Under the leadership of the governor and his chief policymakers, the state has created a planning calendar consisting of a six-month planning and policy cycle during which goals and plans are reviewed and updated, followed by a six-month budget cycle.

Resource Allocation

An organization's resources are not limited to those contained in its annual or biennial operating or capital budgets. In the private sector, the four primary resources are capital, workers, technology and good will. The public sector draws on the same resources, except that good will would appropriately be termed a "political" resource.

Foresight, goal setting and strategic planning set the stage for resource allocations. Unfortunately, these strategic processes are the antithesis of prevailing practices in the public sector. Today, most governments allocate resources by increasing or reducing previous funding levels, with little consideration of the needs, goals and plans of the programs involved. The use of strategic processes ensures that future needs and commitments are not preempted by short-term considerations.

Evaluations

The more influential and pervasive its foresight, goal-setting and strategic planning processes become, the better an organization can evaluate the short- and long-term effectiveness of its policies, programs and managers. However, if the strategic processes are to be effective, they require constant monitoring and regular evaluations. Positive findings give the assurance to continue already planned actions. However if it is found that foresight is faulty, or the goals and strategic plans are inappropriate or operations are deficient, then management can find out why and take appropriate corrective action.

Major companies that engage in strategic processes make annual evaluations of their strategic process. They systematically reassess their foresight conclusions and processes. This permits them to improve their foresight processes and evaluate the current and prospective significance of specific long-term issues. For instance, energy availability was a critical issue to most organizations in 1979; but it was far less so in 1984.

Similarly, many business organizations that engage in strategic processes will review their longer term goals periodically: thereby permitting them to reaffirm those goals that are central to the organization, modify those requiring change, and add new goals. In like manner, the beginning of a new administration (public or private) or the beginning of a renewed term of office for the public CEO is generally an appropriate time to evaluate longer term goals of the institution.

As they reassess their goals, most private companies that engage in strategic processes annually review their longer term strategic plans, assess how next year's actions will fit into that plan and identify what changes (if any) are required. Such attention gives longer term objectives and needs of the organization a closer equality with the heavy demands that always exist for short-term results. It also helps insure that longer term strategies are sound and that the short-term actions fit into a longer term approach. Systematic evaluations also provide a basis for distributing rewards and recognition—which in turn reinforces the importance of thinking strategically.

The absence in government of a bottom line for measuring performance has traditionally been used as an excuse for not using strategic management concepts. Even in the private sector, however, it is difficult to measure and reward strategic actions. Thus, most companies have created compensation packages for their managers that differentiate between managers in growing businesses and those in non-growing businesses. These evaluations are based on common sense criteria that often have little to do with short-term payoffs, but rather are constructed around other measures such as the success in entering specific markets, increasing market shares, recruiting key staff, or reaching agreed upon production levels within specific financial and operational limits.

Developing performance indicators in government presents the same kind of challenge as it does in growing businesses that are not yet making profits. Benchmarks can be designed, however, by simply evaluating performance on the basis of how well short-term actions relate to longer term plans. Such measures can be devised for virtually every unit and subunit of government.

Organizational Culture

An organization's culture is reflected in its formal and informal principles, policies, procedures, values and attitudes. Often, there are enormous differences in organizational cultures, even among companies in the same business. Whatever these differences are, however, the more the organizational culture supports the formal processes of foresight, goal setting, strategic planning, operational management and evaluation, the stronger the organization will be. Understanding the culture of an organization and shaping it to support strategic activities are therefore essential planning and management tools.

However, one basic tenet underlies virtually every corporate culture: if the CEO is not interested in something, then little is usually done. Thus, if the CEO is not openly concerned about implementing strategic processes in the organization, then managers are not likely to devote much time or attention to that effort. But if the CEO is interested and visibly committed to strategic processes, including their use for evaluation and compensation decisions, then managers will not only become responsible for implementing strategic plans, they are also likely to become more aggressively involved in plan development.

Guidelines for Action

Virtually every governmental organization is unique, at least in terms of its culture. Nevertheless, for officials who wish to institute strategic processes, there are some common guidelines that merit consideration:

- Affirm the CEO's commitment to the process and visibly indicate that commitment;
- Define a statement of goals, indicating primary areas of endeavor;
- Strengthen where it exists, and create where it does not, the organizational capacity to identify pivotal structural changes or discrete events that will affect the organization, along with a method to disseminate this information to all organizational units involved in strategic and operational planning;
- Define how the foresight and strategic planning unit(s) will operate—both as entities and in relation to other staff and line functions;
- Create and use a procedure for assessing the relationship between plans of individual organizational units and the overall goals of the organization, and then establish a process for allocating resources accordingly;
- Create a program to train analysts, planners and managers in strategic concepts;
- Create a program to strengthen the planning sensitivity of current and potential managers;

- Create a procedure for reviewing the overall foresight, goal-setting, strategic planning, operational planning and evaluation process and its implications for the organization as a whole; and
- Commit to a strong and systematic evaluation process.

The actions required to introduce, institutionalize, manage and link strategic vision to strategic planning and improved operations do not rely on elaborate models or arcane management techniques. Rather, they are common sense approaches to many actions that public-sector CEOs would take anyway. However, the advantages of explicitly engaging in this strategic process are those that always flow from using systematic rather than ad hoc approaches: namely, emerging opportunities can be better identified and captured and potentially adverse consequences can be better anticipated and minimized.

CHAPTER 5

Conclusion

THE EFFECTIVE MANAGEMENT of any organization, public or private, in a rapidly changing, complex environment is becoming an increasingly difficult challenge. Today, a large number of major American corporations—along with a growing number of leaders in the Congress, federal departments, and state and local governments—are successfully meeting this challenge by creating a strategic vision of their future.

To create that vision and determine how they will get there, organizations in both public and private sectors are instituting the fundamental processes of strategic management: foresight, goal setting, strategic planning, systematic linkages between strategic plans and operations, and evaluations.

Although there are barriers to the introduction of these processes in government, their importance is often inflated to rationalize failure or inaction. When compared with the barriers to effective management in the private sector, the circumstances of government actually appear much more stable. For example, most corporate CEOs must produce annual, even quarterly, results if they are to thwart takeover attempts and retain the confidence of stockholders and board members. A public CEO generally has at least four years in which to conceive and implement a program—a rare luxury in the private sector. Moreover, criticism of the public official is often discounted by the voters as "just politics."

Yet the public CEO's time advantage is no guarantee of successful public administration. With time, but without a strategic vision, a public CEO is likely to become mired in responding to daily organizational crises and the demands of special interests. With the application of strategic vision and strategic management practices, however, it is possible to identify key issues; set an agenda; and simultaneously overcome, even focus, the predictable buffeting of events, the press and special interests.

The long-term payoffs of creating and introducing foresight, goal-setting and strategic planning processes more than compensate for any difficulties that might be encountered in initiating the process. In describing why such processes are important to business, George Steiner notes the following reasons, each of which explains its value to the public sector as well:

- It is indispensable to a top manager's effectively discharging basic responsibilities;
- It simulates the future—on paper. It encourages and permits the manager to see, evaluate and accept or discard a far greater number of alternative courses of action than might otherwise be considered;
- It applies the systems approach to management, thus permitting the manager to see things as part of a whole;
- It reveals and clarifies future opportunities and threats. It helps a manager to foresee new opportunities and then exercise innovative skills in exploiting them. Managers are also in a better position to eliminate or reduce the impact of threats than if they appear unexpectedly;
- It provides an overall framework for decision-making throughout the organization, thus preventing piecemeal decisions and providing a basis for testing value judgments;
- It provides a basis for other management functions, such as the effective use of resources;
- It is a means of communicating objectives, strategies and detailed operational plans to all levels of government;
- It helps managers to master change;
- It develops attitudes, perspectives, ways of thinking, decision-making habits and a planning philosophy that will produce better decisions;
- It provides a basis for measuring qualitative performance. Non-qualitative characteristics such as creativity, innovation, imagination, motivation and knowledge can be assessed.

Thus, strategic processes represent an intellectual framework as well as a set of management practices. The intellectual framework provides the discipline to define specific values and assign priorities to actions. The management practices translate vision into reality.

Today, the processes of strategic vision are an appropriate, timely and necessary response to the challenges raised by Peter Drucker in the conclusion to *Managing in Turbulent Times*:

> Rarely has a new social institution, a new social function, emerged as fast as management in this century. Rarely, if ever, has it become indispensable so fast. But rarely also has a new institution, a new leadership group, faced as demanding, as challenging, as exciting a test as the one that managing in turbulent times now poses to the managements of businesses and non-business public service institutions alike.[20]

Commonly Used Techniques To Improve Government Management

The policy, structural, and administrative disarray in government management practices has not gone unnoticed. Numerous studies have documented this disorder and the resulting administrative confusion and disorientation in the priority-setting processes of organizations in both the public and private sectors. Numerous attempts have been made to streamline the structures and management processes of government to remedy this disarray. The principal attempts are as follows:

Reorganization—One of the most attractive, most often attempted and least successful means of bringing policy and administrative coherence to government operations has been the reorganization of basic institutions. Since 1948, for example, there have been 28 major attempts to restructure and consolidate the federal economic policy-making machinery that is now fragmented among 33 separate departments and agencies *outside* of the Executive Office of the President. These efforts have failed repeatedly.

Government-Sponsored and -Mandated Planning— Public planning, sponsored by the federal government and conducted by subordinate units of government, is a technique often used in efforts to improve policy and administrative focus. Today, there are still over 40 federally sponsored planning programs in the fields of economic and community development, environmental protection, transportation, energy development, social services, public safety, and general policy development and management. Yet as the Advisory Commission on Intergovernmental Relations has concluded, given the absence of overall goals and objectives and ineffective linkages between plans and actions, the introduction of new planning programs has proved an ineffective means of improving the coherence of government actions. Too often government planning is left as a side show in public administration, consuming time, resources and attention but producing few improvements in policymaking and program administration.

Interagency Task Forces and Interagency Agreements —The formation of working groups and task forces composed of appointed and senior career officials is another device long used to coordinate the actions of multiple programs. However, while this approach is useful for dealing with specific problems in the short term, its longer term usefulness is limited. Personalities change too rapidly and institutional memory is too quickly lost. It is most useful as an initiative device for confronting longer term management needs.

Centrally Directed Simplification Efforts—There have been a number of attempts to simplify policy and administrative decisions through massive simplification and process changes. Block grants are a prime example of such efforts. However, shifting the location of management within the federalist system does not necessarily ensure improved management.

The Intergovernmental Consultation Process—Several Administrations have been involved in a long-term effort to ensure that appropriate state and local governments would be involved in a variety of federal decision-making processes that affect them. One means of facilitating such involvement had been the A-95 review process which was administered by the Office of Management and Budget. However, this device only informed. It did not permit formal involvement of state and local governments in actual decision-making. Thus, its impact on improving overall policy and administrative coherence must be rated as limited.

Budgetary Techniques—A variety of budgetary devices have been created to improve the management of government. The better known of these are the Zero Based Budgeting (ZBB) system of the Carter Administration and the Planning, Programming and Budgeting (PPB) system of the Johnson Administration. These systems proved unsuccessful in large measure because their budgetary role (control of expenditures) was used in lieu of more basic management reforms. Since the federal government prepares its budgets on a three-year cycle and operates on a one-year cycle, long-term considerations are virtually impossible if excessive dependence is placed on budgets as a substitute for other management reforms. Moreover, federal budgeting has many fundamental deficiencies, including the absence of a capital budget.

A Selected Lexicon of Foresight, Goal Setting and Strategic Planning

Base Plan—The plan of action that is consistent with the most likely scenario and with the organization's mission and objectives.

Contingency Plan—The backup plan for the organization's base plan. The plan of action taken should the most probable scenario not materialize as envisioned.

Cost-Benefit—The relation between social and economic benefits and social and economic costs associated with the operation of the system under study, including direct and indirect effects and costs.

Cost-Effectiveness—The relationship within an explicit and finite period, such as product life in service, of cost (as measured in dollars and other tangible values) to effectiveness.

Cross-Impact Analysis—An analytical technique for identifying the various impacts of specific events or well-defined policy actions on other events. It explores whether the occurrence of one event or implementation of one policy is likely to inhibit, enhance, or have no effect on the occurrence of another event.

Delphi—An analytical technique using expert opinion and judgment. It consists of a carefully designed series of interrogations using written questionnaires, personal interviews and/or variations of computer conferencing, statistically evaluated information and opinion feedback, while masking the attribution of particular remarks to individual participants.

Econometric Modeling—A form of modeling, usually done with computers, which explores the components and interactions of a given economic system.

Evaluation—The systematic review of the goals, strategies and operations of the institution, plus the preparation of recommendations for needed adjustments.

External Environment—All relevant elements or forces (social, economic, political, technological) external to and having an impact on the organization.

Foresight—Explicit efforts to systematically monitor and analyze long-term trends and issues—economic, technological, demographic, political, social and foreign—that are likely to influence the future environment in which the institution will operate and to examine the implications of those trends on alternative actions the institution may take.

Goal Setting—The explicit definition of the basic aims of the institution.

Internal Environment—All relevant elements or forces within an organization that affect its components.

Operational Management—The translation of goals and strategies into ongoing operations.

Scenarios—Narrative descriptions of alternative futures based on specific assumptions about relevant social, economic, political and technological forces and their interactions.

Strategic Business Unit—Within a corporation, an independently managed cluster or grouping of products with one or more markets that share similar competitive, growth and other risk and earnings potential characteristics.

Strategic Planning—The process of deciding on the resources used to attain the organization's aims, and on the policies that are to govern the acquisition, use and disposition of those resources.

Strategic Profile—A set of characteristics describing the critical qualities of an enterprise within its field of industry (its opportunities, geographic and product line coverage, resources, costs, competitive standing, special circumstances, etc.), and how these characteristics relate.

Tree Diagram—An analytical tool sometimes referred to as a relevance tree. It is a diagrammatic technique for analyzing systems or processes in which distinct levels of complexity or hierarchy can be identified. It may be used to provide a hierarchical representation of the mission, objectives and policies of a corporation.

Trend-Impact Analysis—An analytical technique for evaluating the potential effect of a set of chosen events upon a designated trend.

Wild-Card Scenario—A scenario with very low probability of occurrence, but high potential impact.

APPENDIX C

Foresight Analytical Techniques

98TH CONGRESS
1st Session

COMMITTEE PRINT

{ COMMITTEE
PRINT 98–B

FORESIGHT IN THE PRIVATE SECTOR: HOW CAN GOVERNMENT USE IT?

REPORT OF THE FORESIGHT TASK FORCE

PREPARED FOR THE USE OF THE

COMMITTEE ON ENERGY AND COMMERCE

U.S. HOUSE OF REPRESENTATIVES

January, 1983

STRATEGIC VISION

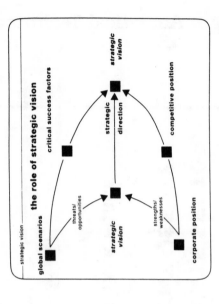

the role of strategic vision

strategic vision

global scenarios

critical success factors

strategic vision

threats/opportunities

strengths/weaknesses

strategic direction

strategic vision

corporate position

competitive position

When faced with meeting the challenge of the strategic future referred to in the August, 1981 report of the House Committee on Energy and Commerce, the private sector typically relies on its strategic management capacities guided by a central strategic vision.

Strategic vision is an explicit, shared understanding of the nature and purpose of the organization. It specifies what the organization is and should be (rather than what it does). As such, it serves as the organization's blueprint for success.

Strategic vision motivates and guides the organization in minimizing the impact of threats and maximizing the benefits of opportunities posed by the external environment. Strategic vision stabilizes the organization in times of turbulence and uncertainty.

In the view of the Task Force, an eloquent statement of national strategic vision was set forth in the Declaration of Independence.

STRATEGIC PROCESS

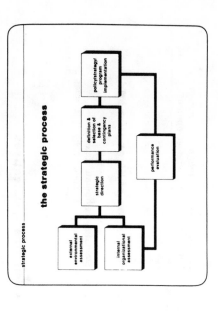

the strategic process

strategic process

- external environmental assessment
- internal organizational assessment
- strategic direction
- definition & selection of base & contingency plans
- policy/strategy/ program implementation
- performance evaluation

The strategic process* used in the private sector generally consists of six building blocks:

- ■ Analysis of the External Environment.
- ■ Analysis of the Internal Environment.
- ■ Direction Setting.
- ■ Definition and Selection of Base and Contingency Plans.
- ■ Implementation.
- ■ Performance Evaluation.

Given that the fundamental challenges are common to both sectors, the same model may be useful in the public sector.

The following summarizes the basic building blocks, while subsequent sections of the report go into greater depth in each area.

*As used in this context, strategic refers to anticipating change and making choices among options which favor the organization's adaptive capacities.

61

Analysis of the External Environment: Identification of Threats and Opportunities

This is the principal area traditionally associated with foresight. It involves judgment concerning alternative outcomes of existing trends as well as speculation about emerging developments. Specifically, it focusses on threats and opportunities.

Analysis of the Internal Environment: Identification of Strengths and Weaknesses

This involves self-assessment in which the organization evaluates its human, financial, technological and structural/informational capacities and potentialities. Specifically, it focuses on the organization's strengths and weaknesses.

Direction Setting: Specification of Mission, Goals, Objectives

The strategic process is usually embedded within a vision which provides guidance for the organization. Direction setting renders this vision concrete in terms of defining an operational mission, goals and objectives.

Definition and Selection of Base and Contingent Plans

This part of the process involves identification of alternative courses of action under alternative future conditions.

Implementation

Usually, this activity involves accountability and execution.

Performance Evaluation

Performance evaluation compares actual with expected results and identifies the reasons for and magnitude of differences.

NETWORKING

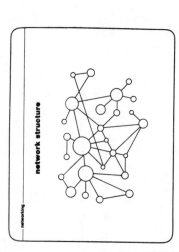

When confronted with needs similiar to those outlined by the House Committee on Energy and Commerce, the private sector typically employs a network model. (The Foresight Task Force itself is a network.)

A network is "a collection of individuals and/or organizations loosely and voluntarily linked with one another for a variety of mutually beneficial exchanges including ideas, information, resources and/or personnel."** Instead of depending on traditional, hierarchical forms of organization, a network depends on informal, interdependent structures which evolve over time and can easily ignore bureaucratic and institutional boundaries in executing their mission.

Constituent elements of the strategic process are summarized on pages 65-81.

ENVIRONMENTAL ASSESSMENT

Environmental assessment usually involves one or more of four activities:

- ■ Scenario Construction.
- ■ Premises Quantification.
- ■ Monitoring.
- ■ Scanning.

There is no rule that all four must be used, or used in the order specified.

Scenario Construction

Scenarios are comprehensive, internally consistent narratives describing a variety of plausible futures. Usually, they are based on assumptions concerning complex interactions among international, regional, domestic and/or local social, economic, political and technological influences.

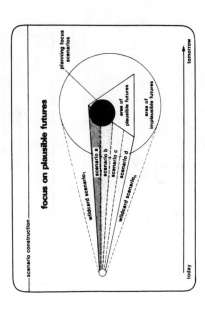

scenario construction

scenario development process

key strategic issues/decisions

key decision factors

strategic implications

scenario logics

scenarios

critical environmental forces

monitoring scanning

scenario construction

alternative scenarios

inter'l political/ economic conditions	major political thrusts	
	centralization (country-building)	decentralization (region-building)
muddling along	scenario a	scenario b
restructured growth after crisis	scenario c	scenario d

Scenarios are useful because they provide an explicit and realistic frame of reference for the key forces/ uncertainties that may impinge on specific strategic issues and/or decisions. The objective of scenario construction is to develop a planning focus against which to evaluate strengths and weaknesses, make base and contingency plans and allocate resources.

The first step in scenario construction is the identification of key strategic issues and/or decisions. The next step is the identification and analysis of key variables affecting these issues and/or decisions. Typically, this leads to the specification of a variety of scenario logics encompassing the main driving forces critical to the outcome of the issues and/or decisions. These logics give the scenarios distinct thrusts and directions distinguishing each from the others, thus facilitating the formulation of specific, but flexible, base and contingency plans. The third and final step in the scenario construction process is the identification of strategic implications, i.e. the threats and opportunities implied by each scenario. This information, when combined with the results of self assessment (strengths and weaknesses), leads to the identification of leverage points where the organization's plans may be expected to be maximally effective in defining and accomplishing desired goals and objectives.

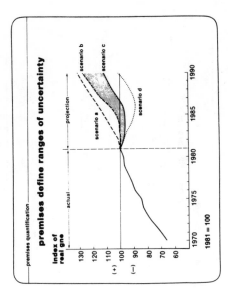

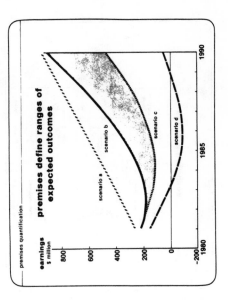

Premises Quantification

Once the scenarios' logics and main driving forces are identified, key variables (usually expressed as time series trends) can be projected for each scenario by use of tools and techniques, such as trend impact, cross impact, delphi, extrapolation, econometric modelling, etc.

An example of premises quantification and its relationship to scenario construction is shown in illustrations to the right. From among this company's four scenarios, two have been selected for base and contingency planning purposes (scenario b and c.) Key variables, i.e. factors of major strategic significance such as economic performance, as measured by gne, and corporate earnings, are then forecast according to the assumptions applicable in each of the two planning focus scenarios. The result is a bounded range of outcomes within which direction setting, policy and strategy formulation and resource allocation planning can take place.

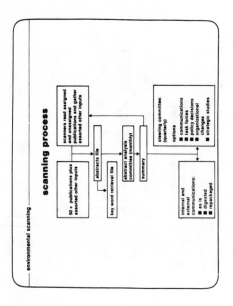

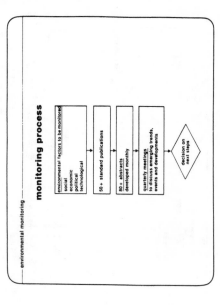

Scanning/Monitoring

Environmental scanning may be best likened to a radar screen where random signals are registered which an observer then analyzes for possible pattern formation.

Environmental monitoring may best be likened to an electrocardiogram where the behavior of known variables is tracked or monitored for actual vs anticipated performance.

Two approaches to scanning and monitoring are widely used in the private sector. These are illustrated to the right. While these approaches represent the commercially available products of a particular consulting house, they are descriptive of the procedures generally undertaken by the private sector irrespective of whether that consulting house is involved.

ORGANIZATIONAL ASSESSMENT

There are four separate, but related resource assessments a company typically carries out on itself: These evaluate the organization's strengths and weaknesses in the areas of:

- People.
- Money.
- Technology.
- Information.

Human Resource Assessment

This assessment usually involves a comparison of the skill base required by the strategic direction with that of the existing skill base. The purpose is to ensure that the necessary skill base is or will be in place to fulfill the organization's mission, goals and objectives. In addition to the inventory approach illustrated to the right other approaches involve perception testing of key constituencies which may include such procedures as opinion polls, personal and/or group interviews, surveys and/or group meetings.

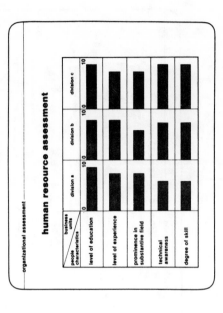

organizational assessment

human resource assessment

people characteristics / business units	division a	division b	division c
level of education			
level of experience			
prominence in substantive field			
technical awareness			
degree of skill			

Financial Assessment

Usually, this assessment involves a series of analyses based on the concept of contribution to corporate value. For application in the public sector, concepts of cost/benefit and cost/effectiveness may be more appropriate.

The illustration to the right shows one company's approach in integrating this series of analyses into a single package. Key elements include (clockwise from upper left):

■ the *corporate value matrix*, showing how growth and profitability combine to determine corporate value, thereby providing a measurement of capability and criterion for choosing among strategic options.

■ the *operating portfolio*, displaying the basic strategic position of the business that determines its profitability potential.

■ the *strategy direction chart*, illustrating the resulting position of selected strategic options.

■ the *financial portfolio*, illustrating levels of expected profitability associated with a business' position in the operating portfolio and its strategic thrust indicated on the strategy direction chart.

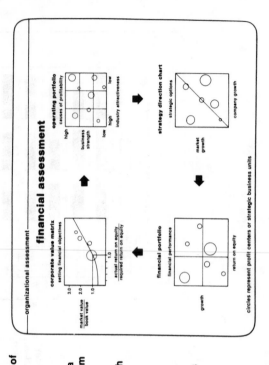

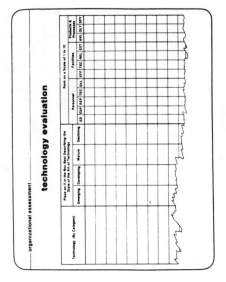

Technology Evaluation

Generally, this assessment, similiar to the human resources assessment, involves an inventory of the organization's existing technology compared with the technology necessary to fulfill the organization's mission, goals and objectives.

Information/Structural Assessment

There are few norms governing this area of self-assessment except that the guiding principle usually has to do with the efficient and effective flow of information for decision-making/strategy implementation purposes. In the private sector, the strategic business unit (sbu, sometimes referred to as a profit center) is usually the organizing principle for this analysis. In the public sector, the concept of accountability center may be a useful substitute.

DIRECTION SETTING

Setting strategic direction typically involves three steps. It is absolutely critical, however, that the organization's senior management participate in and actively lead this three step process. These steps include:

■ Surveying present and prospective realities and potentialities.

■ Identifying and testing alternative directions and profiles including their organizational and operational implications.

■ Deciding on the direction and profile of the organization, periodically reviewing its legitimacy/viability and communicating these in the form of mission, goals and objectives to key stakeholder groups.

Missions, Goals/Objectives

What is meant by mission, goals and objectives is summarized as follows:

■ *Mission:* What the organization is in business to accomplish, e.g. an energy company may be in business of discovering and developing energy resources for the purpose of producing and selling them at a profit.

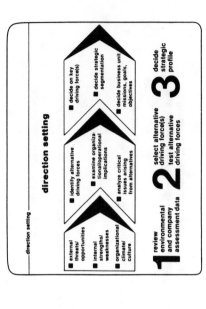

direction setting

direction setting

- external threats/opportunities
- internal strengths/weaknesses
- organizational climate/culture

- identify alternative driving forces
- examine organizational/operational implications
- analyze critical issues arising from alternatives

- decide on key driving force(s)
- decide strategic segmentation
- decide business unit missions, goals, objectives

1 review environmental and company assessment data

2 select alternative driving force(s)
test alternative driving forces

3 decide strategic profile

■ *Goals:* How the organization will carry out its mission, e.g. in the energy example, by pushing the exploration and development business, by maintaining profitable synergistic businesses and by divesting all other businesses.

■ *Objectives:* The specific measures of accomplishment specifying at which levels goals have been met, e.g. key projects must meet an 18-24% financial screening rate.

The product of the three step direction setting process includes:

■ A simple, concise statement of strategic direction adequate to guide both long term decision-making and short term day-to-day operations.

■ A commitment to that direction based on shared understanding throughout the organization and its major stakeholder groups.

■ A basis for policy, plans and program formulation and resource allocation.

■ A basis for identifying and handling critical strategic issues.

IMPLEMENTATION

implementation

Illustrative example: strategy diagram

objective	strategies	programs
revitalize downtown	encourage private rehabilitation of older structures	encourage investor response to federal tax credits
		provide industrial revenue bonds
		reduce development-control risks
		raise demand for quality space
	improve infrastructure and maintenance	allow sale-leaseback of public facilities
		provide efficient fire protection
		impose assessments and user charges
		contract for mechanized trash removal
	improve traffic movement and parking	improve parking management system
		give tax and density credits for private parking development
		seek investment in new transportation forms
	control street crime	create juvenile jobs in architectural rehabilitation
		target tax incentives
		increase foot patrol
		motivate unified way project

The transition from mission, goals and objectives to implementation is frequently facilitated by use of a tree diagram. The illustration to the right, drawn from a recent publication aimed at state and municipal governments, shows only the main branches. Typically, these diagrams are extended to include specific tasks as well as accountabilities and performance measures.

Generally, programs are implemented as follows:

■ Assignment of accountability for accomplishment is made to a particular individual, team and/or department.

■ Milestones of accomplishment and expected results are stated in explicit and measureable terms.

■ Provision for periodic evaluation is made.

■ As with every step in the strategic process, top management signals and periodically reinforces its commitment to the process.

EVALUATION

At a minimum, evaluation in the private sector typically involves:

■ A review of the extent to which strategies and programs have been implemented.
■ A review of actual vs expected results against prespecified goals and objectives.

Generally, three kinds of questions are asked:

■ Did the strategies and programs accomplish the desired goals and objectives within target ranges? If not, what adjustments may be necessary?
■ Are other adjustments required with respect to internal strengths and weaknesses?
■ Are other adjustments required with respect to changing external threats and/or opportunities?

Typically, in the private sector, evaluation and feedback serve as part of the management control system.

ISSUES MANAGEMENT

Issues management is interrelated with and contributes to the strategic process in the private sector. In its foresight dimension, it provides crucial intelligence concerning social, economic, political and technological trends, events and developments affecting the organization's strategic viability. It also establishes an agenda for and a means of marshalling participation in the public policy process when issues relate to that arena.

Specifically, the focus of issues management is strategic issues, i.e. those trends, events and developments which meet three criteria:

■ They could impact the organization's performance.

■ The organization must systematically marshall its collective resources to deal with them.

■ The organization may reasonably expect to exert some influence over their outcome.

---

issues management

key questions

■ what is the probability that a given trend, event or development will become a *major* issue?

■ how great will the eventual impact on the institution be?

■ how likely is the impact to be focussed on the institution rather than diffused over the entire community?

■ when is the issue likely to peak
— near-term?
— medium-term?
— long-term?

■ who are the major players and what position(s) are they likely to adopt?

■ what can the organization do to deal with the issue?

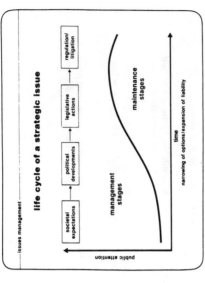

life cycle of a strategic issue

The goal of issues management in the private sector is early warning/early response so that an issue's positive potential can be encouraged/enhanced and its negative potential can be discouraged/inhibited. The objective of issues management is to identify an issue in its early stages of development before options are narrowed and liabilities expanded. *The earlier an issue is identified and dealt with, the more successful the issues management process.*

The notion behind issues management is that issues, like products, industries and even whole societies, are subject to lifecycle principles moving through emerging, developing, maturing and declining stages. Or, as it was once put from the private sector perspective: "The societal concerns of yesterday become the political issues of today, the legislated requirements of tomorrow, and the litigated penalties of the day after."*

*Ian H. Wilson
formerly of The General Electric Company, currently with SRI.

Four Stages of a Strategic Issue's Life Cycle

Within the four stages of an issue's life cycle critical developments occur.

■ *The Societal Expectations stage* signals structural changes, and gives rise to recognition, and often the politicization of an issue.

■ *The Political Developments stage* gives rise to the creation of ad hoc and/or formal organizations to deal with the issue.

■ *The Legislative Actions stage* signals a peak in public attention wherein the issue is defined in operational or legal terms and solutions, frequently in the form of laws and regulations are implemented.

■ *The Regulation/Litigation stage* represents a plateau in public attention when enforcement procedures become routine and penalties apply to those who ignore or violate the spirit, letter and/or intent of the law.

Sufficient foresight in the management stages can lead to organizational actions that may prevent advancement of an issue to the maintenance stages and that, in turn, may disclose positive opportunities for the organization.

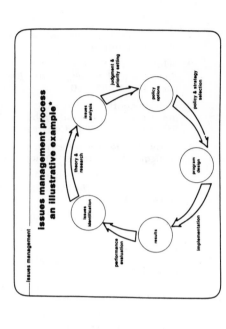

The first step of a typical issues management process in the private sector is environmental and organizational analyses, covered in earlier sections of this report. The second step of the process involves a series of qualitative, sometimes quantitative, analyses evaluating the issues' probability of development, impact and timing. The third step of the process results in a display such as the one to the right where high probability/high impact, (thus, high priority issues) are located in the upper left hand portion of the matrix. In addition to analysis, the issues management process entails development of advocacies that marshall relevant expertise throughout the organization including senior management.

The functional (who does what with whom, when and where) aspects of issues management are perhaps best summarized by the experience of one company whose system is characterized by the double virtues of simplicity and effectiveness. This company's approach is based on a professional staff of issues managers closely linked to both operating units and senior management. Their activities are illustrated in the exhibit to the right.

*Copyright, W. Howard Chase and Barrie L. Jones, 1977 revised.

FOOTNOTES

1. Drucker, Peter F., *Technology, Management, and Society,* Harper Colophon, New York, 1977.
2. Schiff, Frank W., *Looking Ahead: Identifying Key Economic Issues for Business and Society in the 1980s,* Committee for Economic Development, New York, 1980.
3. Congress of the United States, Committee on Energy and Commerce, *Future Opportunities and Problems That Face the Nation,* U.S. House of Representatives, 98th Congress, 1983.
4. Choate, Pat, *Retooling the American Work Force: Toward a National Training Strategy,* The Northeast-Midwest Institute, Washington, D.C., 1982.
5. National Academy of Public Administration, *America's Unelected Government: Recruiting the President's Team,* Ballinger Books, Boston, Massachusetts, 1983.
6. Council of State Planning Agencies, *State Planning,* Washington, D.C., 1976.
7. United States General Accounting Office, *Testimony of the Comptroller General on the Impact of the Senior Executive Service,* Washington, D.C., December 30, 1983.
8. Committee for Economic Development, *Improving the Management of the Public Work Force,* New York, 1977.
9. United States Bureau of the Census, *Statistical Abstract of the United States: 1984* (104th edition.), Washington, D.C., 1983.
10. Choate, Pat and Walter, Susan M., *America in Ruins,* The Council of State Planning Agencies, Washington, D.C., 1981.
11. Choate, *Retooling the American Work Force.*
12. Anthony, Robert N., *Planning and Control Systems, A Framework for Analysis,* Division of Research, Graduate School of Business Administration, Harvard University, Boston, Massachusetts, 1965.
13. Lederman, Leonard L., *Report on a Study of "Foresight" Activities,* National Science Foundation, Washington, D.C., 1983.
14. State of Texas, *Texas Trends,* Texas 2000 Committee, Austin, Texas, 1981.
15. State of Pennsylvania, *Choices for Pennsylvania,* Office of the Governor, Harrisburg, Pennsylvania, 1981.
16. Illinois Budget Office, "The Baby Boom Generation: Impacts on State Revenues and Spending 1950-2025," Springfield, Illinois, 1981.
17. State of Ohio, *Strategic Plan,* Office of the Governor, Columbus, Ohio, 1983.
18. Steiner, George A., *Top Management Planning,* Macmillan Publishing Company, New York, 1969.
19. Steiner, *Top Management Planning.*
20. Drucker, Peter, *Managing in Turbulent Times,* Harper and Row, New York, 1980.

Bibliography

Allio, Robert, J. and Pennington, Malcolm W., *The Politics of Corporate Planning and Modeling*. Planning Executives Institute, Oxford, Ohio, 1978.

――――, *Corporate Planning: Techniques and Applications*, American Management Association, New York, 1979.

Andrews, Kenneth R., *The Concept of Corporate Strategy*, Dow Jones, Homewood, Illinois, 1971.

Ansoff, H. Igor, *Strategic Management*, John Wiley and Sons, Inc., New York, 1979.

Anthony, Robert N., *Planning and Control Systems, A Framework for Analysis*, Division of Research, Graduate School of Business Administration, Harvard University, Boston, Massachusetts, 1965.

Birnbaum, Jeffrey H., "Some Top U.S. Aides Contradict an Image: They Work Very Hard," *The Wall Street Journal*, September 22, 1983.

Blumenthal, Michael, "Candid Reflections of a Businessman in Washington," *Fortune*, January 29, 1979.

Bower, Joseph L. "Effective Public Management," *Harvard Business Review*, March–April 1977.

Campbell, Alan K., "Productivity and Public Management," Remarks to the 11th National Conference on Human Resource Management Systems, October 20, 1980.

Choate, Pat and Walter, Susan, *America in Ruins*, Council of State Planning Agencies, Washington, D.C., 1981.

Choate, Pat, *Retooling the American Work Force: Toward a National Training Strategy*, The Northeast-Midwest Institute, Washington, D.C., 1982.

Coleman, Emily, *Information and Society*, American Telephone and Telegraph Corporation, Basking Ridge, New Jersey, 1981.

Committee for Economic Development, *Improving the Management of the Public Work Force*, New York, 1977.

Commission on the Future of North Carolina, *Summary of Results from Two Surveys About the Future of North Carolina*, 1982.

Congress of the United States, Committee on Energy and Commerce, *Future Opportunities and Problems That Face the Nation*, U.S. House of Representatives, 98th Congress, 1983.

———, *Foresight in the Private Sector: How Can Government Use It?* Report of the Foresight Task Force, January 1983.

Congress of the United States, Subcommittee on Oversight and Investigations, Subcommittee on Energy Conservation and Power, and the Committee on Energy and Commerce, *Public Issue Early Warning Systems: Legislative and Institutional Alternatives*, U.S. House of Representatives, 97th Congress, 1982.

Drucker, Peter, *Managing in Turbulent Times*, Harper and Row, New York, 1980.

———, *Technology, Management and Society*, Harper Colophon, New York, 1977.

Fowles, Jib, editor, *Handbook of Futures Research*, Greenwood Press, Westport, Connecticut, 1978.

Galbraith, Jay R. and Nathanson, Daniel A., *Strategy Implementation: The Role of Structure and Process*, West Publishing Company, St. Paul, Minnesota, 1978.

Goldwin, Robert A., editor, *Political Parties in the Eighties*, American Enterprise Institute, Washington, D.C., 1980.

———, *Bureaucrats, Policy Analysts, Statesmen: Who Leads?* American Enterprise Institute, Washington, D.C., 1980.

Hoch, Standley, "Strategic Management in G.E.," An address to the Annual Meeting of the Council of State Planning Agencies, New Orleans, Louisiana, September 26, 1980.

Illinois Budget Office, "The Baby Boom Generation: Impacts on State Revenues and Spending 1950–2025," Springfield, Illinois, 1981.

King, William R. and Cleland, David, *Strategic Planning and Policy*, Van Nostrand Reinhold Company, New York, 1978.

Lederman, Leonard L., *Report on a Study of "Foresight" Activities*, National Science Foundation, Washington, D.C., 1983.

Levine, Charles H. and Ruben, Irene, editors, *Fiscal Stress and Public Policy*, Sage Publications, Beverly Hills, California, 1980.

Lorange, Peter, *Corporate Planning: An Executive Viewpoint*, Prentice-Hall Inc., Englewood Cliffs, New Jersey, 1980.

Lindbloom, Charles C., *The Intelligence of Democracy*, The Free Press, New York, 1965.

Muchmore, Lynn, "Planning and Budgeting Offices: On Their Relevance to Governatorial Decisions," National Governors Association, 1979.

Moor, Jay H., "Management of Alaska State Government: The Governor's Policy Themes," A presentation at the Annual Meeting of the Council of State Planning Agencies, New Orleans, Louisiana, September 1980.

Missouri Office of Administration, "Overall Program Design and Annual Work Plan," Missouri State Government, Springfield, Missouri, 1980.

Moskow, Michael, *Strategic Planning in Business and Government*, Committee for Economic Development, New York, 1978.

Naylor, Thomas H., editor, *The Politics of Corporate Planning and Modeling*, Planning Executives Institute, Oxford, Ohio, 1978.

National Governor's Association, *Governor's Policy Initiatives: Meeting the Challenges of the 1980s*, Washington, D.C., 1980.

————, *Reflections on Being Governor*, Washington, D.C., 1981.

National Academy for Public Administration, *The Presidency for the 1980s*, Washington, D.C., 1980.

National Academy of Public Administration, *America's Unelected Government: Recruiting the President's Team*, Ballinger Books, Boston, Massachusetts, 1983.

Olsen, John B. and Eadie, Douglas C., *The Game Plan: Governance with Foresight*, The Council of State Planning Agencies, Washington, D.C., 1982.

Olsen, John B., "Applying Business Management Skills to Local Government Operations," *Public Administration Review*, May–June 1979.

Olsen, Raymond T. and Day, Diana H., "Strategic Thinking for State and Local Governments," *Management Focus*, May–June, 1982.

Osgood, William R., *Basics of Successful Business Planning*, the American Management Association, New York, 1980.

Qualls, Robert L., et al., *Corporate Planning: A Guide for Savings and Loan Associations*, United States League of Savings Associations, Washington, D.C., 1978.

Renfro, William, "Congress, Corporations and Crystal Balls: New Partnership for the Future," *Planning Review*, July 1980.

Schiff, Frank W., *Looking Ahead: Identifying Key Economic Issues for Business and Society in the 1980s*, Committee for Economic Development, New York, 1980.

Schwartz, Gail Garfield and Choate, Pat, *Being Number One: Rebuilding the U.S. Economy*, Lexington Books, Lexington, Massachusetts, 1980.

State of New York, *The New York State Economy in the 1980s: A Program for Economic Growth*, Albany, New York, 1981.

State of Ohio, *Strategic Plan*, Office of the Governor, Columbus, Ohio, 1983.

State of Pennsylvania, *Choices for Pennsylvania*, Office of the Governor, Harrisburg, Pennsylvania, 1981.

State of Texas, *Texas Trends*, Texas 2000 Committee, Austin, Texas, 1981.

Steiner, George A., *Top Management Planning*, Macmillan Publishing Company, New York, 1969.

Tregor, Benjamin B. and Zimmerman, John W., *Top Management Strategy: What It Is & How to Make It Work*, Simon and Schuster, New York, 1980.

Thompson, Arthur A. and Strickland, A.J. III, *Strategy and Policy: Concepts and Cases*, Business Publications Inc., Dallas, Texas, 1978.

United States Bureau of the Census, *Statistical Abstract of the United States: 1984* (104th edition), Washington, D.C., 1983.

United States Department of Commerce, *Business and Society: Strategies for the 1980s*, Washington, D.C., 1980.

United States General Accounting Office, *Testimony of the Comptroller General on the Impact of the Senior Executive Service*, Washington, D.C., December 30, 1983.

Vancil, Richard F., "Strategy Formulation in Complex Organizations," *Sloan Management Review*, Winter 1976.

Vancil, Richard F. and Larange, Peter, "How to Design a Strategic Planning System," *Harvard Business Review*, September–October, 1976.

Walter, Susan M., editor, *Proceedings of the White House Conference on Strategic Planning*, Council of State Planning Agencies, Washington, D.C., 1980.

Warren, Charles P., "The States and Urban Strategies: A Comparative Analysis," The National Academy for Public Administration, Washington, D.C., 1980.

Index

DATE DUE